REVIEW OF THE FLEETS

Above: Northrop Grumman

THE US NAVY'S fleet of nine CVN-class aircraft carriers and their respective air wings undertake deployments to the Mediterranean Sea, Red Sea, South China Sea, and the Indian Ocean from their home ports on America's Atlantic and Pacific coasts, and from Japan. The composition of each air wing differs; some feature the E-2D model of Northrop Grumman's Hawkeye radar plane with the F-35C Lightning II stealth fighter and the CMV-22B Osprey providing carrier onboard delivery. Those are deemed air wings of the future because all three types are embarked. Most of the carrier-air wing teams have sailed in the dangerous waters of the Red Sea, menaced by

missile attacks by the Houthis operating in Yemen. Some of the statistics for those deployments are eye opening – from the amount of food consumed by the crew to the number of sorties flown. A detailed account for each air wing makes interesting reading, accompanied by amazing deckside images.

Of equal interest is the 2025 Aviation Plan issued in January by Lieutenant General Bradford Gering, Deputy Commandant for US Marine Corps Aviation. We provide a narrative to the report which covers all aircraft, helicopter and tiltrotor types flown by the service. The MQ-9B Reaper unmanned air system is featured in detail, providing insight to the technologies and mission sets flown by the type. The AV-8B Harrier jump jet

will retire from US Marine Corps service in 2026, so a detailed overview of the ops of the last two squadrons is included,

We also feature an extensive section on the fascinating TACAMO mission held in the past by EC-130 Hercules, the current Boeing 707-based E-6B Mercury (the largest aircraft ever operated by the US Navy), and in the future the nascent E-130J Phoenix II.

This edition covers or touches on most types flown by the US Navy and US Marine Corps, and the service's most interesting missions.

Mark Ayton

Mark Ayton, Editor

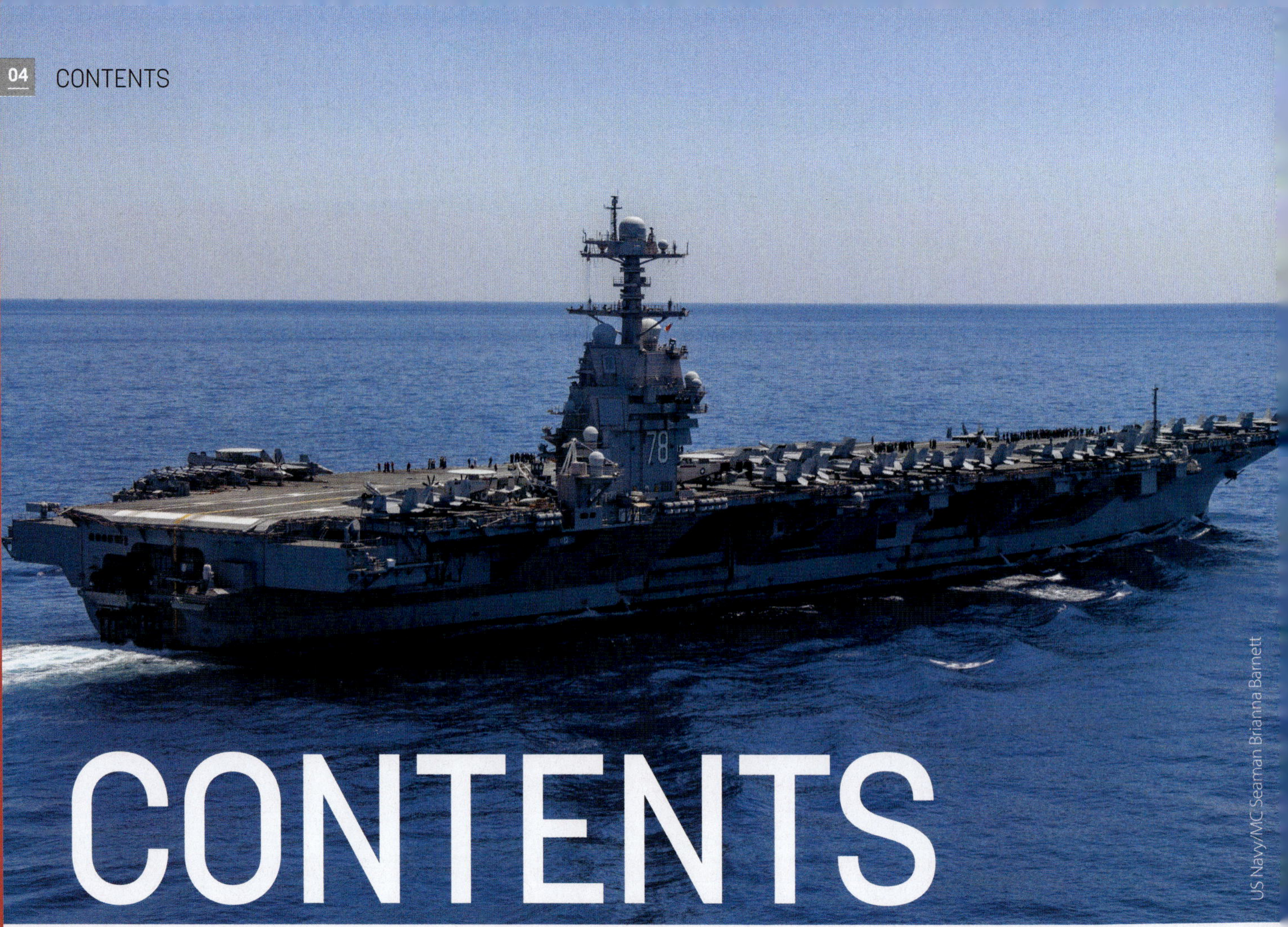

CONTENTS

US Navy/MC3 Alexander Kubitza

US Navy/PO3 Andrew King

ISBN: 978 1 83632 150 7
Editor: Mark Ayton
Senior editor, specials: Roger Mortimer
Email: roger.mortimer@keypublishing.com
Cover Design: Steve Donovan
Design: SJmagic DESIGN SERVICES, India
Advertising Sales Manager: Sam Clark
Email: sam.clark@keypublishing.com
Tel: 01780 755131
Advertising Production: Becky Antoniades
Email: Rebecca.antoniades@ keypublishing.com

SUBSCRIPTION/MAIL ORDER

Key Publishing Ltd, PO Box 300, Stamford, Lincs, PE9 1NA
Tel: 01780 480404
Subscriptions email: subs@ keypublishing.com
Mail Order email: orders@ keypublishing.com
Website: www.keypublishing.com/shop

PUBLISHING

Group CEO: Adrian Cox
Publisher: Steve O'Hara

Published by

Key Publishing Ltd, PO Box 100, Stamford, Lincs, PE9 1XQ
Tel: 01780 755131
Website: www.keypublishing.com

PRINTING

Precision Colour Printing Ltd, Haldane, Halesfield 1, Telford, Shropshire, TF7 4QQ

DISTRIBUTION

Seymour Distribution Ltd, 2 Poultry Avenue, London, EC1A 9PU
Enquiries Line: 02074 294000.

We are unable to guarantee the bona fides of any of our advertisers. Readers are strongly recommended to take their own precautions before parting with any information or item of value, including, but not limited to money, manuscripts, photographs, or personal information in response to any advertisements within this publication.

KEY Publishing

SIXTH-GENERATION F/A-XX

An insight into the US Navy's proposed sixth-generation fighter – the replacement for F/A-18 Super Hornets

TWENTY-THREE YEARS HAVE passed since the editor first visited Strike Fighter Squadron 122 (VFA-122) based at Naval Air Station Lemoore, California. Out on the squadron's massive ramp were three lines of F/A-18 Super Hornets, the first examples of which were delivered from the Boeing St Louis factory in November 1999. Having followed the Super Hornet programme ever since, and written extensively about the type, the Super Hornet is a familiar and favoured jet. The type still stays in my mind as a new fighter aircraft, but that's only partly true. Hundreds of Super Hornets remain in active service with Strike Fighter Squadrons (VFAs) based not only at Lemoore, but also Naval Air Station Oceana, Virginia, and Marine Corps Air Station Iwakuni, Japan. Some of those jets are getting tired and need to be retired from the fleet. Replacing such a large force of fighter aircraft is an exciting prospect for America's three big aircraft manufacturers, Boeing Defense, Lockheed Martin, and Northrop Grumman.

That requirement first broke cover back in 2008. Dubbed the F/A-XX programme, the US Navy (USN) issued a Request for Proposals to industry in the middle of FY2012. The specification was a multi-role strike fighter, capable of air-to-air, air-to-ground, electronic attack, surface attack, close air support within high-threat environments. The USN wanted its F/A-XX to have stealth and super cruise characteristics and equipped with a high-performance radar and a suite of sensors likely capable of reading your car number plate from 100 miles away, and of course, the ability to land aboard and catapult launch from an aircraft carrier. A formidable set of requirements that represents a cost of billions of dollars.

Requirements

By Q2 FY2021, USN officials assigned to the F/A-XX programme office, an organisation established in 2020, released more details on the requirements for F/A-XX.

Firstly, the programme, named Next Generation Air Dominance (NGAD, a

Below: **An artist's impression of a Northop Grumman future fighter parked on the forward deck of an aircraft carrier.** Northrop Grumman

mirror of the US Air Force equivalent sixth-gen programme) would be a family of systems (FoS) in which the aforementioned F/A-XX would be the centrepiece manned fighter aircraft. That family would include unmanned elements, an adjunct air-to-air platform, an adjunct (electronic warfare) platform, even perhaps a platform to succeed the E-2D Advanced Hawkeye airborne early warning and control aircraft. Credentials that fully align the NGAD programme with the USN's vision for future air wings to comprise at least 50% unmanned aircraft.

Second, the F/A-XX element would comprise two increments, each with a different objective. Increment one was to determine the Super Hornet replacement and increment two was to assess a follow-on platform for the EA-18G Growler electronic attack aircraft.

Quarterback

Written testimony by USN officials to the Senate Armed Services sea power subcommittee in March 2022 read: "The NGAD [family of systems] will replace the F/A-18E/F Block II aircraft as they begin to reach end of service life in the 2030s and leverage Manned-Unmanned Teaming (MUM-T) in order to provide increased lethality and survivability.

"F/A-XX is the strike fighter component of the NGAD FoS that will be the 'Quarterback' of the MUM-T concept, directing multiple tactical platforms at the leading edge of the battlespace."

Written testimony by other USN officials to the House Armed Services Subcommittee on Tactical Air and Land Forces read: "The idea for NGAD is that a family of manned and unmanned systems will work together, centred around F/A-XX,

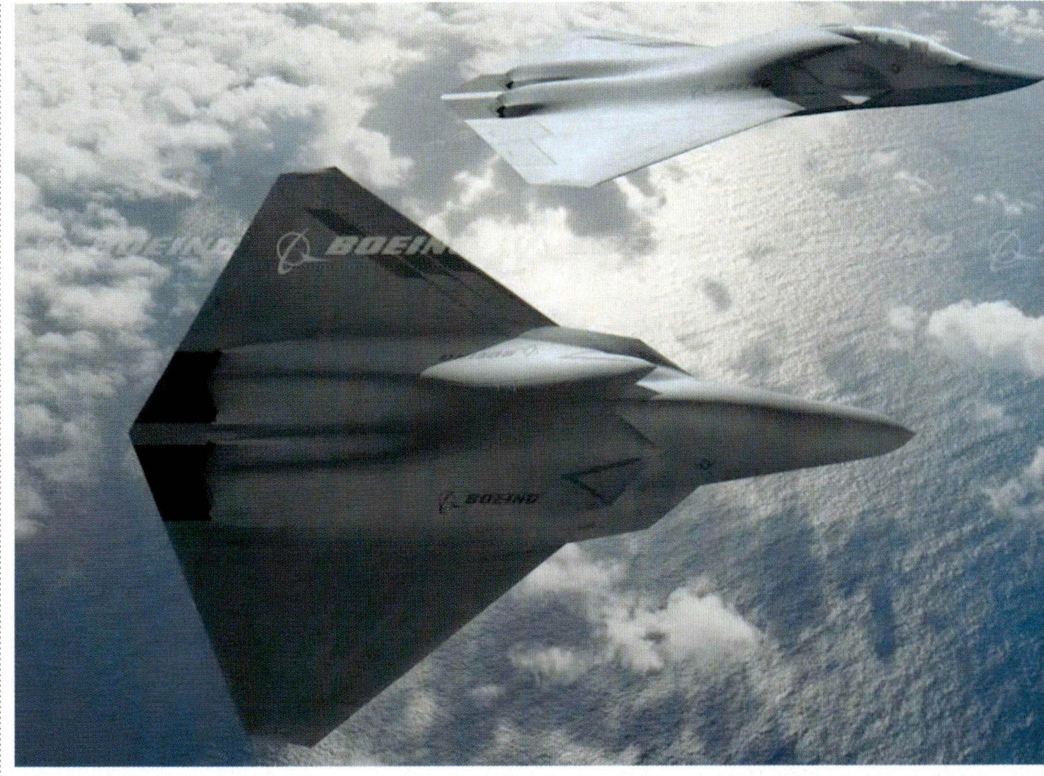

Above: **A Boeing Defense artist's rendering showing two future fighters in its vision of F/A-XX.**
Boeing Defense

which is expected to be a manned fighter. These manned and unmanned aircraft, plus attritable assets, will be employed across domains to enable integrated kinetic and non-kinetic fires at tactically relevant ranges."

A paragraph from a document titled *US Navy Aviation Vision 2030-2035* published by the US Navy in 2022 read: "F/A-XX's specific capabilities and technologies are under development, however analysis shows it must have longer range and greater speed, incorporate passive and active sensor technology, and possess the capability to employ the longer-range weapons programmed for the future. As the Super Hornets are retired from service, a combination of F-35C and F/A-XX will provide Navy tactical fighter aircraft capability and capacity within the CVW."

Budget reduction

President Donald Trump entered office in January 2025, and by June his administration had decided not to continue with F/A-XX and requested just $74m in the USN's FY2026 budget. This is minimal development funding allocated to complete the design of F/A-XX. Trump has funded the USAF F-47 NGAD with a $3.4bn request, an attempt to get the F-47 programme right and to maintain the option for funding F/A-XX in the future. Perhaps a sensible decision, given the Department of Defense's $1 trillion budget.

the contract terms, Northrop Grumman is responsible for integration of the TACAMO mission systems on each C-130J.

The contract includes three Engineering Development Model aircraft with options for up to three more dubbed System Demonstration Test Articles, and up to six aircraft in the first production lot. This corroborates with USN FY2025 budget request documents that call for procurement of six TACAMO aircraft in FY2028, and a further six in FY2029.

Suppliers Lockheed Martin (C-130J aircraft) and Collins Aerospace (VLF transmit system), as subcontractors, will support the integration and airworthiness efforts.

Integration of a secure interface communications system between the cockpit and the mission payload section, critical flight deck avionics systems hardened for nuclear and cyber survivability requirements, and automated flight control system updates, are all included in the contract.

At the time of the contract announcement, Northrop Grumman said it had invested more than $1bn on advanced modelling, digital twin technologies, advanced manufacturing, and agile design, capabilities that assist in

Above: **An artist's rendering of an E-130J aircraft from a different angle, which will relieve the E-6B Mercury of the TACAMO mission.** Northrop Grumman

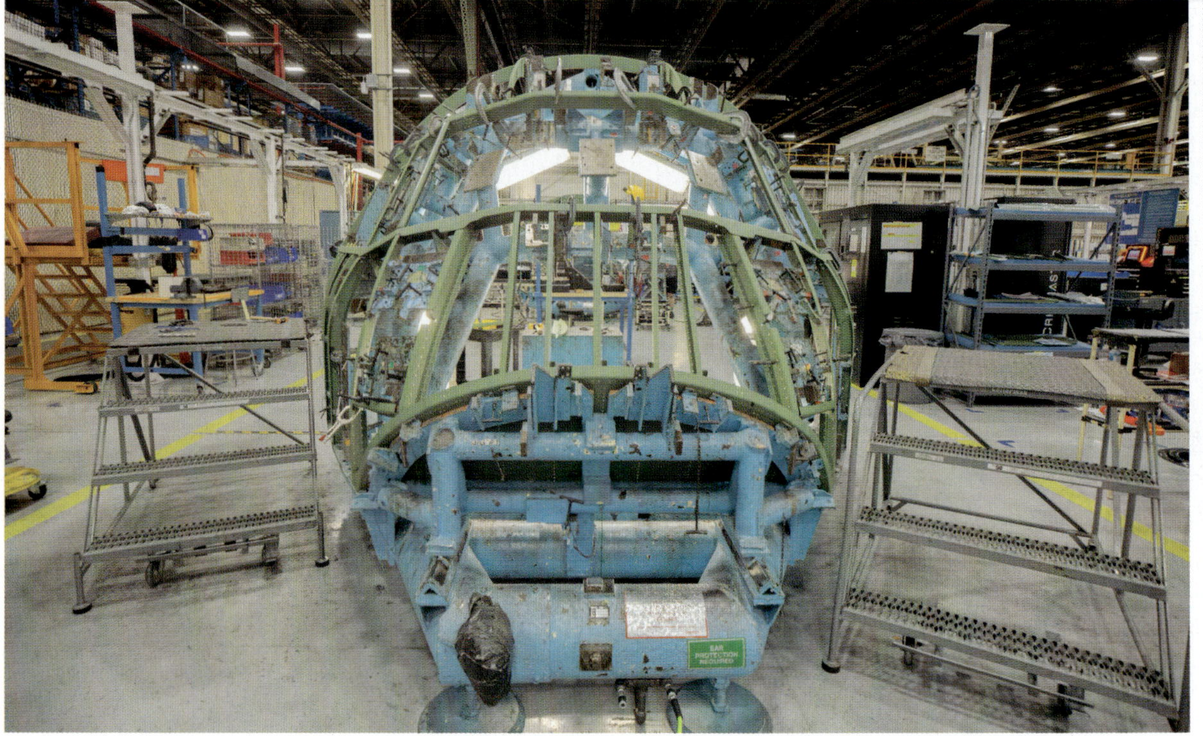

Left: **The first of three C-130J-30 aircraft being built by Lockheed Martin for the USN's E-130J programme. The E-130J, formerly called E-XX, will be the successor to the E-6B Mercury for the TACAMO mission.** Lockheed Martin/ David Key

Above: **The first C-130J-30 aircraft being built by Lockheed Martin for the USN's E-130J programme. This aircraft – the first of three – is planned to be delivered to Naval Air Systems Command in 2026 for modification into an E-130J Engineering Development Model.** Lockheed Martin/David Key

rapidly designing, building, testing, and sustaining the E-130J.

The first aircraft is expected to be delivered to Naval Air Systems Command in 2026 for modification into an EDM-configured E-130J.

The contract award was the result of a competitive source selection that included significant engagement with industry. PMA-271 selected the winner based on the proposal that offered the best value to the government, with consideration given to the offeror's technical approach and cost.

According to NAVAIR: "The E-130J is a critical part of the United States' nuclear modernisation programme, which includes new Columbia-class ballistic missile submarines, new B-21 bomber aircraft, and Sentinel, a new ground-based system to replace the silo-based Minuteman III intercontinental ballistic missiles. The E-130J will ensure that the NCA can always communicate with US nuclear forces to order or cancel strikes, even if ground-based communications are unavailable."

For those readers old enough to remember, between 1963-1993, the TACAMO mission was conducted by a fleet of 20 C-130s designated as EC-130G (four modified C-130E aircraft) and 16 EC-130Q models.

On August 7, 2025, NAVAIR's PMA-271 and Naval Air Force, Pacific's Strategic Communications Wing 1 (SCW-1) announced the name of the new E-130J as the Phoenix II, a reflection of the mythical bird with the ability to be reborn and as a symbol that represents immortality, resurrection, and renewal.

The announcement also confirmed that the E-130J fleet will be assigned to SCW-1 based at Tinker Air Force Base, Oklahoma, where the current E-6B fleet is based.

In the announcement, Captain Roger Davis, PMA-271 programme manager said: "The dedicated team at PMA-271 have committed to the ideals of TACAMO's critical deterrence mission and are transforming the E-6B's capabilities into a new weapon system with unmatched survivability and longevity for this country."

EC-130G and EC-130Q TACAMO

By 1963 outmoded methods of US submarine communications were of concern to the USN and Department of Defense and required a solution. Finding such a solution fell to Rear Admiral Bernard Roeder, Director of Naval Communications, who proposed using the concept of airborne communications, that was deemed high-risk with considerable technological risk. Roeder tasked Lieutenant Jerry Tuttle to implement the proposed concept. At the end of a meeting in which Tuttle was tasked with setting up survivable communications to new submarines armed with Polaris missiles, Roeder said to Tuttle: "That's all, lad, now Take Charge and Move Out." Tuttle had written down many a note from the meeting including a scribbled down acronym for the Admiral's order, that acronym read TACAMO.

According to a January 2008 article titled, *TACAMO – The Survivable Finger on the Trigger* by Jamie Bisher on the excellent Naval Submarine League website: "TACAMO initially took flight with a Lockheed KC-130 Hercules shanghaied from the US Marine Corps. Engineers equipped the aircraft with a very low frequency (VLF) radio transmitter and sent it to communicate with the subsurface force. The experiment succeeded, and, as a result, four US Air Force (USAF) C-130Es were diverted from the Lockheed production line to the USN, designated C-130Gs, and stuffed with a roll-on/roll-off van of strange communications hardware. In 1966 the USN expanded the TACAMO programme. As a result, eight new EC-130Q aircraft with fixed communications suites were ordered, and a new unit, Fleet Air Reconnaissance Squadron 4 (VQ-4), was established at Naval Air Station Patuxent River, Maryland."

The C-130G made the type's service entry in December 1963. Initially all four C-130Gs (later EC-130Gs) were assigned to TACAMO components within Fleet Tactical Support Squadron 21 (VR-21) based at Naval Air Station Barbers Point, Hawaii, and VR-1 based at Naval Air Station Patuxent River, Maryland.

On July 1, 1968, Fleet Air Reconnaissance Squadron 3 (VQ-3) and VQ-4 were commissioned at Naval Air Facility Agana, Guam, and Naval Air Station Patuxent

Above: **EC-130Q BuNo 156172 parked on the flight line at Naval Air Station Barber's Point, Hawaii.** USN

River respectively. During its tenure at Agana, VQ-3 was tasked with maintaining at least one aircraft airborne for 12 hours each day.

Once the squadron was moved to Barbers Point in 1981, its TACAMO posture changed to around-the-clock coverage in an attempt to eliminate the possibility of a Soviet submarine missile attack during the hours when all EC-130 TACAMO aircraft were on the ground leaving the United States without a survivable communications link to its nuclear submarines.

Like most weapon systems, TACAMO underwent a series of upgrades. Its first iteration (TACAMO I) was developed and installed on US Marine Corps KC-130F BuNo 149806. TACAMO II was the first operational version which comprised of three self-contained roll-on roll-off mission system vans which could be installed on board an EC-130G in about five hours.

The third iteration (TACAMO III) was permanently installed on EC-130Q aircraft and featured a five-mile-long trailing antenna and 25kW of transmitting power for the VLF band. TACAMO III was improved to TACAMO IV standard with 200kW of transmitting power and a dual trailing wire antenna system. With TACAMO IV, the EC-130Qs were able to adopt an airborne communication centre role. Also included in the TACAMO III and IV standards were a high-speed reel system for the trailing wire, a message processor system, wing-tip satellite communication antenna pods and electromagnetic pulse hardening to protect the aircraft's circuits and avionic components from radiation.

The EC-130Q model was similar in configuration to the C-130G model with the TACAMO mission as its principal role. Lockheed flew the first airframe, BuNo 156170, in November 1967 followed by USN acceptance and service entry in December and March 1968 respectively.

The EC-130Q featured facilities for flight crew, main fuselage air conditioning and pressurisation, an ARC-132 HF radio, APN-59B radar, APN-153 doppler and ASN-41 main computer. Powered by four Allison T56-A-16 engines each spinning four Hamilton Standard 13ft 6in propellers, the horsepower generated by the four engines was sufficient to lift a regular combat weight of 106,231lb up to a maximum take-off weight of 155,000lb.

Other systems included an integral ramp and cargo door, a thermal de-icing system for the leading edge of the wing and empennage, single point refuelling, an auto pilot, two external under wing 1,360-gallon fuel tanks and high energy brakes. The latter were used when the aircraft was landing on short runways or landing strips such as those found at forward bases. EC-130Qs could use eight Aerojet 15KS-1000 Mk6 JATO jets each rated at 1,090lb to provide additional thrust for take-off from short runways or landing strips. The acronym JATO means Jet Assisted Take-Off.

According to the official USN documentation about the EC-130, a TACAMO's mission profile was:

- Start engines, warm-up, take-off, accelerate to climb speed
- Fly for five minutes at max continuous power at sea level

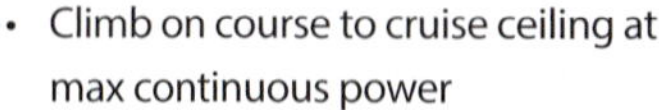

Above: An E-6B Mercury aircraft assigned to Strategic Communications Wing 1 (SCW-1) taxis along the runway at Offutt Air Force Base, Nebraska. UASF/ SSgt Jacob Skovo

- Climb on course to cruise ceiling at max continuous power
- Cruise to station at speeds and altitudes for max range
- Climb to 25,000ft
- Loiter at 25,000ft at maximum continuous power in tight orbits to enable the trailing-wire antenna to droop in a near vertical position to optimise how VLF radio waves penetrate water most effectively
- Climb on course to cruise ceiling at maximum continuous power
- Cruise to home base at speeds and altitudes for maximum range
- Land at home base with fuel reserve.

The fuel reserve enabled 30 minutes of flight as rated at sea level and speeds for max endurance plus 5% of initial fuel.

Carrying a max fuel payload of 59,269lb with a 25,000lb payload, an EC-130Q had a 1,000nm combat radius with a 10.39-hour mission time when flying at an average 286kts cruise speed at up to 28,500ft.

After 30 years of keeping a silent watch and for almost 20 years of that timeline flying every hour of every day, USN EC-130G and EC-130Q TACAMO aircraft were retired from service in August 1993. Their role was taken over by a fleet of 16 Boeing E-6A Hermes aircraft configured for both TACAMO mission and the ABNCP/Looking Glass role, previously the mission performed by the EC-135-series family of aircraft in support of Operation Looking Glass, operated by wings assigned to USAF's Strategic Air Command. Looking Glass facilitates the launch of US land-based intercontinental ballistic missiles using an airborne launch control system.

E-6B Mercury

Originally configured for the TACAMO survivable nuclear communications role and designated as the E-6A Hermes, each aircraft was upgraded to E-6B Mercury standard to conduct the ABNCP mission. The first E-6B model was delivered back to the USN in late 1997.

An E-6B can also backup and relay communications for a Boeing E-4B National Airborne Command Center aircraft, (based on the Boeing 747-200), four of which are operated by the USAF's 55th Wing based at Offutt Air Force Base, Nebraska.

Mercury Fleet

The E-6B is the heaviest aircraft ever operated by the USN. Manufactured as Boeing 707-320 models between 1988 and 1991, the 16 E-6B aircraft were the last 707 models built. All but one of the 16-aircraft fleet is now assigned to Strategic Communications Wing 1 (SCW-1) based at Tinker Air Force Base, Oklahoma, under the control of US Strategic Command (STRATCOM). SCW-1 assigns two aircraft to stand alert duty at staging bases: one at Travis Air Force Base, California, and one at Naval Air Station Patuxent River, Maryland.

E-6B MAIN SYSTEMS

- ALCS used for programming and launching ICBMs and SLBMs.
- ALR-66(V)4 electronic support measures sets housed in each wingtip pod.
- ARC-190 HF radio with wingtip and vertical fin HF probe antennas.
- Very-Low-Frequency (VLF) high-power transmission system rated at 200kW, which transmits through retractable 28,000ft or 5,000ft trailing-wire antennae housed in the tail cone. Flying at a bank angle of between 25° and 40°, one of the two antennae hangs vertically to enable the VLF signal to penetrate water and reach a submarine's trailing cable antenna. The airframe was purposely reinforced against the sustained stresses imposed by sustained periods of flying at a banked angle.
- UHF radio used for Command, Control, and Communication that uses Frequency Division Multiplexing, a technique that allows multiple signals to be transmitted simultaneously over a single communication channel by dividing the available bandwidth into different frequency ranges.
- All systems are hardened against electro-magnetic pulse, so communication remains operational during a nuclear conflict.

The E-6B operates across a wide frequency spectrum to transmit and receive secure and non-secure voice and data information as part of the TACAMO strategic communications mission. The aircraft provides survivable, endurable, reliable airborne command, control, and communications in support of the President, Secretary of Defense, and United States Strategic Command.

At a tactical level, SCW-1 is assigned two operational squadrons, one fleet replacement squadron, a weapons school, and fleet introduction team. The fleet replacement squadron runs training courses for pilots, naval flight officers, and flight engineers. After their course, aircrew undertake follow-on training in highly specialised disciplines such as advanced tactics and weapon systems employment and nuclear command-and-control certification.

Founded in July 2019, the TACAMO weapons school conducts the Naval Air Warfare Development Center's mission of training advanced tactics, techniques, and procedures across assigned combat mission areas at the individual, unit, and integrated and joint levels. Its mission aligns with the training continuum; to set and enforce combat proficiency standards.

The weapons school is also responsible for crew certification and warfare development efforts for the TACAMO and ABNCP/Looking Glass mission sets and supports the development and integration of new capabilities into E-6B aircraft assigned to SCW-1.

Fleet Air Reconnaissance Squadron 3 (VQ-3) 'Ironmen', and VQ-4 'Shadows' are the operational squadrons,

Above: **A member of the 625th Strategic Operations Squadron, reads a technical order book sat in front of the Airborne Launch Control System procedures trainer at Offutt Air Force Base, Nebraska.** USAF/ Charles Haymond

and VQ-7 'Roughnecks' is the fleet replacement squadron.

The fleet introduction team provides operational input to testing, evaluation, and preparation training for operating the aircraft with modifications. Its objective is to bridge the gap between operating the jet under test conditions and front-line operations. The fleet introduction team also manages and ensures transition of all modifications without stand-down.

An E-6B mission crew can number up to 22, usually including six USAF personnel who fly as members of the battle staff. These airmen are assigned to Air Force Global Strike Command's 625th Strategic Operations Squadron (STOS).

According to the 625th, it has two primary one-of-a-kind mission focus areas: the Airborne Launch Control System (ALCS) and ICBM targeting. The ALCS is an integral part of the Minuteman III ICBM weapon system and is meant to be a 'survivable' means for launching ICBMs. ICBM targeting, received from USSTRATCOM, is transmitted, via force direction messages, to ICBM forces.

The 625th STOS provided the following details of its six unique flights:

The ALCS Combat Operations Flight provides combat forces for STRATCOM's ABNCP on board the E-6B Mercury aircraft. Flying as members of the battle staff, the ALCS crew, using on-board equipment, can launch ICBMs. Additionally, members provide intelligence, ad-hoc targeting, missile warning, battle damage assessment, and ballistic missile defence support for the on-board airborne emergency actions officer (AEAO).

Left: **A test conductor-airborne and a deputy missile combat crew commander-airborne, assigned to the 625th Strategic Operations Squadron, work through missile launch procedures prior to an operational ICBM test launch.** USAF/A1C Keifer Bowes

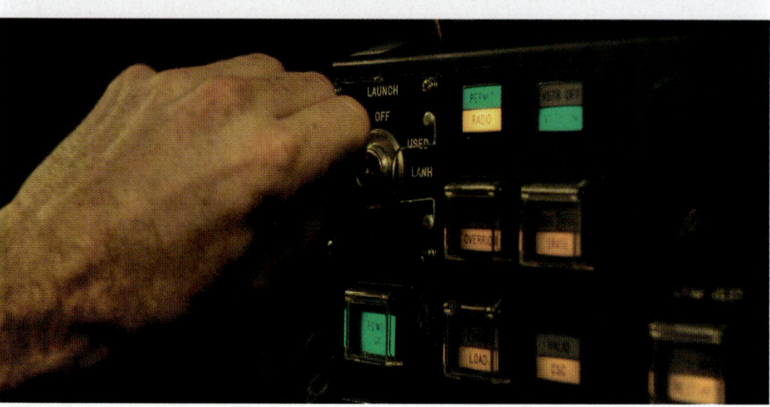

Left: **A deputy missile combat crew commander launches a simulated Minuteman III missile while aboard a E-6B Mercury.** USAF/ A1C Keifer Bowes

Above: **An E-6B Mercury awaits take-off at Vandenberg Space Force Base, California on October 31, 2023.** USAF/SrA Joshua Carroll

Right: **An analysis engineer monitors the status of a simulated Minuteman III missile from aboard a E-6B Mercury.** USAF/ A1C Keifer Bowes

An ALCS Training and Evaluation Flight trains and supports airborne missileers who operate the ALCS onboard the E-6B, as well as those who conduct ALCS test and analysis missions.

A Test and Analysis Flight plans and executes flight safety zones and optimum weapon system launch tracks for the ALCS onboard the E-6B aircraft. This flight also oversees flight performance analysis and capability assessments of US and foreign ballistic missile weapon systems. Additionally, the flight is designated as the airborne test conductor for ICBM force evaluation missions in which it leads, plans, and co-ordinates test missions of the ALCS with STRATCOM, Air Force Global Strike Command, the USN, and other US agencies.

An ICBM targeting flight, working with STRATCOM and 20th Air Force, maintains targeting for the US fleet of 450 ICBMs. It also conducts targeting and range safety analysis for all ICBM test launches and supports software testing by Air Force Global Strike Command. Finally,

it develops, documents, verifies, and maintains all targeting software programs and operating procedures required for daily ICBM alert operations.

The ICBM targeting systems flight develops, documents, verifies, and maintains the operational readiness for ICBM targeting software programs and operating procedures required for daily Minuteman III targeting operations. It also provides direct support to the other five flights within the 625th, with software development, programming operations, and sustaining the networks.

A weapons and tactics flight is responsible for instructor training: developing tactics, techniques, and procedures, and operational certification for both the targeting and ALCS missions. It also supports integration of ALCS and ABNCP mission sets into one combat-ready force to facilitate wartime and targeting operations with Air Force Global Strike Command's Minutemen III-equipped missile wings based at F E Warren, Wyoming, Malstrom, Montana, and Minot, North Dakota.

Sustaining the Fleet

Discussing the sustainment strategy used for the E-6B fleet of aircraft, Captain Adam Scott, NAVAIR's former E-6B programme manager said: "PMA-271 provides the US

Right: **The stylish lines of the Boeing 707 seen in the form of an E-6B Mercury.** Dan Stijovich

Above: **A deputy missile combat crew commander-airborne from the 625th Strategic Operations Squadron, goes over pre-launch procedures aboard a US Navy E-6B Mercury.** USAF/ A1C Keifer Bowes

Below: **A US Navy E-6B Mercury strategic airborne command post aircraft takes off from Offutt Air Force Base, Nebraska.** USAF/ Josh Plueger

Navy's component of airborne command, control, and communications capability required to ensure the president is constantly able to reach his nuclear forces: bombers, missile fields, and submarines. We always need to have the E-6B aircraft ready to accomplish their mission."

PMA-271's role is challenging given the E-6B fleet's age. Partnerships with industry and the Naval Air Enterprise are key to its work, not least with smaller companies that are now conducting some of the work once completed by the larger defence companies.

Outlining the service life for an E-6B aircraft, Scott said: "When the aircraft came off the production line [as Boeing 707-320 models] in the late 1980s, they had a service life of 25,000 hours. We've performed a service life assessment programme and completed a service life extension programme out to 45,000 flight hours.

According to NAVAIR, E-6B aircraft are projected to reach their 45,000-hour service life between 2038 and 2040.

The service life assessment showed a series of issues such that PMA-271 is now performing the Service Life Extension Program 1B, to address issues that were previously unaffordable.

Explaining the effort, Scott said: "We accommodate the service life extension work into the aircraft's heavy maintenance periods undertaken at the USAF Air Logistics Center at Oklahoma City [the depot]. As the aircraft get older, the number of man hours worked during heavy maintenance continues to increase.

"Individual aircraft tracking systems are another part of our strategy to sustain the aircraft for as long as we can. The current 45,000-hour service life is based on engineering math and estimation. We outfitted two E-6B aircraft with strain gauges and data monitoring for a two-year process of data collection. We input aircraft fatigue life data, as measured, into our models, and undertook analysis. We hope the results will give us more service life if needed, but it will better inform our decisions as we get further and further through the life of the aircraft."

PMA-271 has a reliability control board, as per the type used by the airline industry comprising a team of experts from within the Naval Aviation Enterprise, which is evaluating how corrosion prevention can be improved. PMA-271 staff visited Southwest and Delta, to see how reliability control boards operate. Scott said: "It's a very methodical process within which we evaluate what the issues are and assemble cross-functional teams to solve the problems."

Parts Manufacture

According to NAVAIR, corrosion and stress corrosion cracks were discovered on E-6B spar chords during in-service and depot maintenance. The material used to make the original spar chords is obsolete, so in addition to evaluating alternate corrosion prevention treatments, PMA-271 had to also qualify a new material.

Explaining the process, Scott said: "Through partnerships with Boeing and some of its sub-vendors, we determined how to change the original materials to a new alternate material. The spar chords were originally manufactured with a specific grade of aluminium, so we procured the last stocks of that aluminium grade and undertook

considerable engineering work to get an alternate material approved."

To achieve that objective, PMA-271 had to oversee new manufacturing processes so vendors could produce new parts. The Boeing 707 design was detailed on 2D drawings, a media no longer used by vendors for parts production. Consequently, PMA-271 had to convert 2D drawings into 3D computer models and its staff had to devise a new method of manufacture the engineering for which was challenging.

After months of work, the first newly manufactured spar chord was delivered to the depot at Tinker in the summer of 2021 based on the increasing number of spar chords requiring replacement, combined with predictive determinations of further replacements, to increase the low number in stock, PMA-271 had to contract manufacture of new spar chords.

Scott said PMA-271 is working with Vertex Aerospace, its contract logistic support agent which uses a tool set for predictive analytics. "This will help us to find ways to use our data to predict when spar chords need replacing. We are also working with Boeing for its expertise in individual aircraft tracking systems, to work through the data, and determine ways to predict what's going to be next."

Additive manufacturing is also being used to produce replacement parts. An example is the aircraft's fuel dump manifold which was originally a cast component.

According to NAVAIR, in September 2021 a fully qualified additively manufactured water separator was

approved for use on E-6B aircraft. New units are replacing legacy separators, which had been a top concern for PMA-271 and the depot since early 2020.

Giving other examples of component replacement, Scott said: "During depot inspections we uncovered some heat damage caused by the auxiliary power unit [APU] fitted to the Block I-configured aircraft, so we're also upgrading the APU to provide the aircraft with more power and more cooling capacity. Both outputs are essential for the communication systems onboard. As the number of aircraft fitted with the new APU increases, the required number of maintenance man hours required for repairs to heat damage will decrease, and aircraft mission capability rates should increase."

According to PMA-271, there are no pending obsolescence issues for the

Above: **An E-6B Mercury refuels from a KC-135R Stratotanker assigned to the 507th Air Refueling Wing based at Tinker Air Force Base, Oklahoma.** UASF/ Greg Davis

E-6B flight deck, yet programme staff are planning for a future flight deck modernisation and are awaiting results from a Boeing study on the E-6 cockpit.

First Block II Under IMMC

On June 6, 2023, Northrop Grumman announced that the first E-6B Mercury aircraft upgraded under the IMMC had been delivered back to the USN.

Northrop Grumman was awarded the Integrated Modification and Maintenance Contract (IMMC) for the USN's E-6B Mercury aircraft in February 2022. Work was performed at Northrop Grumman's Aircraft Maintenance and Fabrication Center in Lake Charles, Louisiana.

PMA-271 began the herculean task of upgrading each of its 16 E-6B

BLOCK I UPGRADE

The E-6B Block I upgrade was undertaken by Collins Aerospace at its aircraft modification and operations facility at Will Rogers Airport in Oklahoma City. It was focused on the aircraft's communication suite.

According to ARINC Engineering Services, subcontractor to Rockwell Collins, work included comprehensive removal, upgrade, and replacement of receivers, transmitters, communications racks, and operator stations that support the aircraft's central communications and battle staff suites.

The E-6B Block I programme started in 2004, achieved initial operational capability declaration in 2014, and the last aircraft upgraded was delivered back to the USN in October 2020. The upgrade included:

- Battle staff workstations upgraded with interlinked MCS-10 computers, the core of the communication system upgrade.
- Enhanced electrical power and cooling systems to power and cool the new equipment.
- Large dorsal radome fitted on the upper forward fuselage, housing antennae for the Military Strategic Tactical and Relay (MILSTAR) satellite communication and UHF radio system.
- Internet Protocol Bandwidth Expansion upgrade to improve internet access to information onto, off, and throughout the aircraft.
- Onboard secure network for message processing, communications control, and monitoring.
- Open system architecture for mission avionics.
- Voice Over Internet Protocol intercommunications system.

Mercury aircraft in 2017, but quickly found that taking the planes out of service for 475 days – the average turnaround time for the first two Block II modifications completed – was not sustainable. It needed a faster way to deliver the required capabilities to the fleet.

Initially three installers were responsible for the six engineering change proposals (ECPs) required for Block II. They include a combination of mission systems upgrades and aircraft sustainment initiatives.

PMA-271's solution was to integrate the six ECPs into one Block II modification contract and implement new practices, including one called performance to plan, to transform the process. Consequently, PMA-271 awarded the IMMC to Northrop Grumman in February 2022 and inducted the first aircraft under the agreement in May 2022, 90 days ahead of the contract schedule.

Northrop Grumman delivered that aircraft in a record 392 days, followed by another record of 255 days on the second plane, which it delivered on October 24. The turnaround time (TAT) required by the IMMC is 180 days, a goal that was expected to be met with the third aircraft.

"We must achieve our target turnaround time in order to ensure our squadrons have enough mission-ready aircraft equipped with the upgraded communications capabilities that they require," said PMA-271 programme manager Scott. "Every organisation involved in producing a Block II aircraft is collaborating, identifying and solving problem areas, and setting aggressive goals to accomplish this no-fail mission, and we are seeing results."

The six ECPs included in Block II will provide more secure, modernised communications systems.

Above: **A 55th Security Forces master at arms stands watch near an E-6 Mercury on the flightline at Offutt Air Force Base.** USAF/Josh Plueger

Below: **An avionics technician and an electrician assigned to Fleet Air Reconnaissance Squadron 3 (VQ-3) wait for an E-6B Mercury aircraft to taxi onto its parking spot at Offutt Air Force Base, Nebraska.** USAF/TSgt Chris Thornbury

Until the E-6B's successor, the E-XX (E-130J) is delivered, the E-6B must be mission-ready. The fleet is vital to the military's nuclear command, control, and communications at a time when Russia, China, North Korea, and Iran are increasingly vocal about their nuclear capabilities.

Scott said the best way for the United States to deter its adversaries from using nuclear weapons is by assuring them that "we are always ready and willing to respond".

IMMC Explained

When PMA-271 began upgrading E-6B aircraft in 2017, three separate entities completed the work at Waco, Texas, but without any of the three empowered to drive schedule and performance, resulting in delays.

PMA-271 leadership moved to an IMMC with the goal of reducing delays by setting aggressive goals – including the 180-day TAT – embracing a performance to plan mindset and improving collaboration between the entities involved. It was the first time a single company had assumed responsibility for the entire installation, reducing bureaucracy and improving speed.

Northrop Grumman conducts the upgrades from its Aircraft Maintenance and Fabrication Center (AMFC) in Lake Charles, Louisiana. The $111m IMMC covers the remaining 12 aircraft in the fleet and is scheduled for completion by 2026.

The Block II modification team comprises Northrop Grumman, V2X, PMA-271 and

BLOCK II UPGRADE

The E-6B Block II upgrade programme is progressing well following the implementation of the IMMC contract to an industry team led by Northop Grumman.

The upgrade includes:

- Advanced Extremely High Frequency beyond-line-of-sight terminals and voice conferencing for communications to the NCA.
- Northrop Grumman-installed multi-role tactical common data link (MR-TCDL) with SATCOM capability two Ku band line-of-sight channels and one Ka satellite communications channel.
- New dorsal and ventral radomes.

Left: **An aviation machinist's mate airman working inside a virtual E-6B Mercury using a new multi-purpose reconfigurable 3D panel trainer at Tinker Air Force Base, Oklahoma.** USN/ Chief Petty Officer Jeremy Jones

Fleet Readiness Center Southeast at Naval Air Station Jacksonville, Florida. The team embraced the USN's 'get real, get better' initiative focused on improving organisational performance and fostering a culture of continuous improvement to deliver required capabilities to the fleet as quickly as possible.

Commenting on the imitative, Bob Stailey, the E-6B deputy programme manager at the time said: "The Block II team aggressively tackled the challenge of improving the Block II modification process and their success is demonstrated by the downward trend in turnaround times. This wouldn't have been possible without their creative thinking and fully embracing the get real, get better practices."

The team implemented process improvements that span engineering, scheduling, management, and production. They improved production control on the modification line, streamlined engineering dispositions, increased support manning, and established an executable integrated master schedule aimed at achieving the 180-day deadline.

They established a weekly meeting, known as a heads-up display (HUD), bringing all the organisations together to report on their performance in real time, elevate barriers and workshop solutions. The HUD format improves accountability by assigning individual ownership and deadlines for specific tasks. Regular reporting of real-time data allows the team to identify and solve problems early before they cause delays. It also ensures everyone is aligned on goals and expectations.

Scott said: "The HUD demonstrates performance to plan in action. The team embraced the Naval Aviation Enterprise guiding principles and, over time, developed the trust required to openly discuss performance shortfalls and address them as a team. They established clear plans and measured performance to those plans weekly. The frequency of their interactions and the wide dissemination of information accelerated decision-making and barrier removal. By applying the 'get real, get better' principles, the Block II modification team is expediting increased capability to the fleet."

FRCSE provided engineering, production artisans and logistician personnel in support of the E-6B Block II modification. The artisans included sheet metal workers, electricians, machinists, non-destructive inspectors, and planners. All told, FRCSE contributed 26 personnel and more than 8,700 hours of work to help bring the vital upgrade to a national strategic asset.

The IMMC also provides maintenance flexibility. In addition to the six Block II ECPs, the contract provides options for Northrop Grumman to perform depot-level in-service repairs (ISRs) as needs arise. This saves time and money – especially on critical ISRs that ground an aircraft – and improves overall fleet readiness. For example, under the IMMC, Northrop Grumman was able to quickly repair a cracked tail on one of the aircraft undergoing a depot event at Tinker Air Force Base.

Below: **An E-6B Mercury lands at Offutt Air Force Base, Nebraska during a simulated electronic minuteman test flight, September 17, 2024.** USAF/ TSgt Chris Thornbury

Members of PMA-271 and Northrop Grumman employees pose in front of the first E-6B Mercury aircraft inducted to Northrop Grumman's Lake Charles, Louisiana facility under the Integrated Modification and Maintenance Contract IMMC which sought to decrease average turnaround times from 19 months to six months. *Northrop Grumman*

Virtual Training System

On July 22, 2024, NAVAIR announced details of virtual 3D training systems used to train USN E-6B operators and maintainers.

NAVAIR's PMA-271 delivered the new Multi-Purpose Reconfigurable Training System (MRTS) to Tinker Air Force Base, Oklahoma, during Q1 FY2024, followed in August by the Mission Avionics System Trainer (MAST) for E-6B mission systems operators. The systems are produced by Florida-based Proactive Technologies Inc and JHT Inc.

The MRTS and MAST projects were a collaboration between PMA-271 and PMA-205, NAVAIR's Naval Aviation Training Systems and Ranges Program Office, the Center for Naval Aviation Technical Training, and the Naval Air Warfare Center Training Systems Division.

MRTS maintenance trainers, and a third system called the Virtual Checklist Trainer are designed to improve training, reduce risk, and save money by providing hands-on instruction in a classroom rather than on the aircraft. They allow maintainers and operators to train for the mission, even when fleet aircraft are unavailable due to operational requirements.

Discussing the systems in a release, Barry Polk, NAWCTSD programme manager and PMA-271's training lead said: "The classrooms are a controlled environment and allow for a higher

Right: **Students practice conducting maintenance on an E-6B Mercury using a new multi-purpose reconfigurable 3D panel trainer at Tinker Air Force Base, Oklahoma.** USN/ Chief Petty Officer Jeremy Jones

Right: **Crew members assigned to the 625th Strategic Operations Squadron, work onboard a USN E-6B Mercury aircraft at Vandenberg Space Force Base, California, on October 31, 2023.** USAF/SrA Joshua Carroll

E-6B MERCURY CHARACTERISTICS

Wingspan	148ft 4in
Length	150ft 4in
Stabiliser span	45ft 8in
Height	42ft 5in
Endurance	13½ hours
Endurance with air refuelling	72 hours
Max gross weight	342,000lb
Max speed	Mach 0.88
Ceiling	42,000ft
Range	6,600nm with six-hour loiter time
Powerplant	Four CFM-56-2A-2 high-bypass turbofan engines each rated at 24,000lb

instructor-student ratio. The generation entering the fleet now are more adept at these 3D environments. They're already comfortable in the virtual world, it will speed up training and give them better training."

The newest system, the MRTS 3D panel trainers, are interactive simulators that model and provide troubleshooting scenarios for various aircraft systems. They replace the original panel trainers from the 1980s, which were designed for the E-6A Hermes fleet before it transitioned to the E-6B configuration. The massive panels were stagnant, outdated and no longer replicated the actual E-6B aircraft.

The MRTS simulates the fuel flow, electrical flow, auxiliary power unit, hydraulics, environmental control system, and pre- and post-flight checklists. Students use either a touch-screen panel or videogame controller to interact with the system. They can practice getting into the body of the aircraft, opening panels, and conducting maintenance, with all the proper maintenance processes embedded.

Polk explained: "They're in a nice classroom that's not dependent on aircraft availability or weather. And, of course, if they do something wrong, it doesn't down the jet."

Instructors and students began using the new system in January 2024, including as part of the month-long organisational level maintenance course.

Below: **This top-down shot of an E-6B clearly shows the large dorsal radome fitted on the upper forward fuselage, housing antennae for MILSTAR satellite communication and wing-tip antenna pods.** USAF/Greg Davis

Describing the MRTS, Center for Naval Aviation Technical Training (CNATT) instructor Coy Weese said: "Students get to experience the next best thing to working on the actual aircraft in a safe and controlled training environment where mistakes can be made and learned from without damage to equipment or injury to personnel. With MRTS we can repeat the training over and over as many times as necessary to ensure the information is retained, and we can drive home the severity of completing all maintenance with the 'by the book' mentality which ensures the job was done right the first time every time."

Discussing their experiences of using the MRTS, students said the system prepared them for working on the aircraft by providing hands-on, interactive training. Aviation Machinist's Mate Airman Maribel Lopez said: "I knew where the auxiliary power unit was located before I even saw the aircraft in-person."

And Aviation Machinist's Mate Airman Logan Gottschalk said: "It was very helpful in seeing how the hydraulics, electrical, and fuel systems work; it was more in-depth."

The VCT provides virtual training for crew that operate the two very low frequency trailing wire antennas that extend two-and-a-half miles and five miles behind the aircraft, respectively, to enable TACAMO message transmissions to submarines.

The USN uses the MRTS for training on other systems, including the Tomahawk missile launch console and submarine community support system. The MAST works in a similar way to the MRTS, but provides training on how to check out, troubleshoot, and isolate faults, and how to remove and replace components for the communications, battle staff and receiver-transmitter equipment.

HARRIER
BEFORE SUNDOWN

An overview of the US Marine Corps' dwindling AV-8B fleet, including final flights and aircraft retirements.

ON FEBRUARY 3, 2025, Lieutenant General Bradford Gering, Deputy Commandant for Marine Aviation unveiled the US Marine Corps (USMC's) 2025 Aviation Plan. In the section about the AV-8B force, Gering said: "The AV-8B's lethality and V/STOL [vertical/short take-off and landing] capability, combined with an Amphibious Ready Group's proximity to coastal targets, rapid turnaround time, and hot weapons reloading, make it uniquely suited for deployment on Marine Expeditionary Units [MEUs].

"The inventory comprises 25 AV-8Bs assigned to Marine Attack Squadron 223 (VMA-223) based at Marine Corps Air Station Cherry Point, North Carolina, which will sundown in late FY2026.

"An AV-8B squadron maintains six to seven aircraft deployed on MEUs, with an additional six to 12 aircraft in workup until the platform's operational sundown in FY2026. AV-8B structure requirements will remain in place until the end of FY2026."

All AV-8B pilot and maintainer training is complete and all remaining operations will be supported by VMA-223.

Discussing the AV-8B's configuration, Gering said: "Final weapons, sensors, and survivability upgrades have been implemented and will remain relevant for the aircraft's remaining time in service... Until the end of FY2026, the AV-8B

Above: An AV-8B Harrier assigned to Marine Attack Squadron 231 (VMA-231) approaches an MC-130J Commando II assigned to Air Force Special Operations Command before aerial refuelling during Exercise Emerald Warrior 25-1 in Arizona, on February 6, 2025. USAF/SSgt Tyler McQuiston

community will continue to support the training of forward air controllers, and joint terminal attack controllers, and fulfil service-level tasks in the United States and overseas."

The last two AV-8B Harrier II+, VMA-223 and VMA-231 will both transition to the F-35B as Marine Fighter Attack (VMFA) squadrons. VMA-231 'Ace of Spades' made its final AV-8B Harrier II flight on May 29, culminating decades of history and distinguished service with the iconic VTOL.

Ace of Spades

First commissioned in 1919, VMA-231 is the USMC's oldest flying squadron and has served with distinction in multiple conflicts worldwide. After equipping with the AV-8B Harrier II in 1985, VMA-231 supported major operations to include Operations Desert Shield, Desert Storm, Allied Force, Odyssey Dawn, Inherent Resolve, and most recently, Prosperity Guardian in the Red Sea.

The squadron's final flight and colours casing ceremony took place at Marine Corps Air Station Cherry Point and represented a significant milestone in the ongoing fifth-generation tactical aircraft transition. Attendees included marines and sailors assigned to VMA-231, their families, and veterans who had previously served with the squadron. Major General William Swan, commanding general of the 2nd Marine Aircraft Wing (MAW), and Major General James Wellons, commanding general of the 3rd MAW, as well as several distinguished guests, community leaders and former commanding officers of the squadron were also there.

Lieutenant Colonel Paul Truog, VMA-231's commanding officer at the time, and Sergeant Major Christianna Wolford, oversaw VMA-231's official deactivation in September 2025. The squadron is due to reactivate as Marine Fighter Attack Squadron 231 (VMFA-231) in FY2026. As VMFA-231, the squadron will continue the unit's storied legacy with fifth-generation capabilities as an F-35B Lightning II squadron.

Many of the marines assigned to VMA-231 will continue to serve as F-35 pilots and maintainers across the USMC.

The squadron's transition from the legacy AV-8B Harrier II to the F-35B Lightning II is part of the 2nd MAW's ongoing modernisation effort. As the aviation combat element for the MEU, the 2nd MAW continues to balance modernisation with providing combat-ready aviation forces.

Fort Worth's Harrier

On May 13, AV-8B II+ Harrier, BuNo 165357, was inducted into the Fort Worth Aviation Museum located at Fort Worth Meacham International Airport, Texas.

The aircraft was flown from Marine Corps Air Station Cherry Point to Meacham by Captain Zach Moore assigned to VMA-231. Upon arrival, Moore performed a fly-by at the observation area before vertically landing.

Ben Guttery, the museum's collections manager said: "This aircraft's extensive combat history is very important to us and will be greatly appreciated by the

Above: AV-8B Harrier IIs assigned to Marine Attack Squadron 231 (VMA-231) fly in formation during the squadron's ceremony to celebrate its last Harrier flight before its deactivation in September at Marine Corps Air Station Cherry Point, on May 29, 2025. USMC/LCpl Bryan Giraldo

public. The AV-8B II+ will eventually be bookend displayed next to the AV-8A, demonstrating the many changes of the Harrier from when it first went into service with the US Marines."

AV-8B BuNo 165357 entered USMC service as a day attack variant on September 16, 1985. It was stricken, remanufactured and re-entered service on June 12, 1998, as an AV-8B Harrier II+. It was operated by VMA-223, VMA-231 and VMA-542, accumulating 8,955 flight hours, including 995 combat flight hours in support of multiple Marine Expeditionary Unit deployments, Operation Iraqi Freedom, Operation Enduring Freedom deployments, and humanitarian efforts.

Harriers Head West

On June 10, three AV-8B Harriers took off from Marine Corps Air Station Cherry Point, each bound for new homes in the west of America. After two aerial refuellings, the aircraft split formation near Albuquerque, New Mexico, and headed for their individual destinations: Buckley Space Force Base, Colorado, Mesa Field, Arizona, and Marine Corps Air Station Yuma, Arizona. A team tasked with demilitarising each aircraft flew on a KC-130J on a nine-day cross country mission to prepare the aircraft for display. Their first stop was Buckley followed by Mesa and then Yuma

Retired in the Rockies

AV-8B BuNo 165587 was piloted across the country to the Wings Over the Rockies Air & Space Museum at Buckley Space Force Base near Denver, Colorado, by Captain Ryan Gettinger.

It arrived on June 12 with a fanfare, rich history, and a legacy of innovation.

An AV-8B takes off on a close air support mission during Exercise Southern Strike 2023, a joint multinational exercise aimed at improving interoperability among allies and branches of the US Department of Defense. USMC/Cpl Christian Cortez

A KC-130, loaded with tools and carrying a demilitarisation team, arrived a few hours later. The team worked on the aircraft to configure it as a safe exhibit for the museum.

AV-8B BuNo 165587 entered USMC service in 1987 as a day attack variant before being remanufactured into a Harrier II+ in December 2000. Over the course of its service life, it was operated by VMA-211, VMA-214, VMA-513, VMA-311, and finally VMA-231, and amassed over 8,900 flight hours, including 1,436 hours in combat in support of Operation Iraqi Freedom, Operation Enduring Freedom, humanitarian missions, and Marine Expeditionary Unit deployments.

Commemorative Air Force

AV-8B Harrier II+ BuNo 165576 landed at Falcon Field in Mesa, Arizona on June 10, marking the aircraft's official retirement and its induction into the Commemorative Air Force (CAF) Airbase Arizona Museum.

Major Robert Weede flew the AV-8B from Marine Corps Air Station Cherry Point. On June 13, the USMC demilitarisation team arrived at the CAF facility after travelling from Buckley Space Force Base in Colorado.

AV-8B BuNo 165576 entered USMC service in 1987 and was later remanufactured to AV-8B Harrier II+ standard in 2000. It operated with multiple squadrons including VMA-214, VMA-311, and VMA-231, accumulating more than 8,200 flight hours, including over 1,200 in combat supporting US forces in Iraq and Afghanistan.

Alan Urban, museum director and curator at CAF Airbase Arizona said: "It's not every day you get to witness the last chapter of a legendary aircraft written live in your own hangar. This Harrier tells a story of power, precision, and perseverance."

Back to Yuma

On September 14, 2012, Taliban insurgents attacked Camp Bastion, destroying multiple Harriers on the flight line and tragically killing US Marines Sergeant Bradley Atwell and Lieutenant Colonel Christopher Raible.

AV-8B Harrier II+ BuNo 165588 was the only aircraft damaged in the attack that was fully repaired and returned to service. The aircraft had been on static display at Marine Corps Air Station Yuma since June 2021 in honour of Atwell and Raible.

On June 10, the aircraft was flown to Yuma by Lieutenant Colonel Paul Truog, commanding officer of VMA-231. Aircraft 165428 has taken the place of aircraft 165588 as Yuma's Harrier static display while aircraft 165588 will be displayed at

Above: **Marines with the Marine Attack Squadron 231 (VMA-231) colour guard stand at parade rest during the squadron's final AV-8B Harrier II flight ceremony at Marine Corps Air Station Cherry Point on May 29, 2025.** USMC/LCpl Bryan Giraldo

Left: **AV-8B Harrier II+ BuNo 165428 parked at Marine Corps Air Station Yuma, Arizona, on June 10, 2025, after the jet's final flight.** USMC/LCpl Hannah Dodson

Above: **An AV-8B Harrier II+ assigned to Marine Attack Squadron 231 (VMA-231) uploads fuel from an MC-130J Commando II assigned to Air Force Special Operations Command during Emerald Warrior 25-1 in Arizona, February 6, 2025.** USAF/SSgt Tyler McQuiston

the Smithsonian's Udvar-Hazy Center near Washington DC.

AV-8B Harrier II+ BuNo 165428 was operated by VMA-223, VMA-231 and VMA-542, accumulating over 9,000 flight hours, including 1,364 combat flight hours in support of multiple operations.

The AV-8B Harrier II+ was used by the Royal Air Force and Royal Navy, the USMC, and the Italian and Spanish naval air arms. Designed by the British to operate in austere environments, in service with the USMC, Harriers supported expeditionary air operations for over 40 years.

Its mission set included close air support, armed reconnaissance, defensive counterair, and interdiction.

The journey of the aircraft on June 10 from USMC service to the role of museum centrepiece was made possible through a multi-agency collaboration including the AV-8B Harrier Program Office (PMA-257), Headquarters, USMC, Marine Aircraft Group 14 (MAG-14) based at USMC Air Station Cherry Point, and marines from Marine Attack Squadron 231 (VMA-231).

AV-8B Carrier Qualification

AV-8B squadrons deployed six to seven aircraft as part of a MEU embarked onboard a US Navy amphibious assault ship dubbed an LHD (landing helicopter dock). A critical event for each LHD during its pre-deployment workup cycle is the certification of the ship's flight deck for aviation operations.

Between December 2-6, 2024, more than 30 marines from the 22nd MEU embarked on USS *Iwo Jima* (LHD 7) successfully completed numerous landings and take-offs in collaboration with the US Navy's Afloat Training Group to meet certification requirements for flight deck operations.

AV-8B Harriers assigned to VMA-223 were embarked onboard the *Iwo Jima*. To achieve carrier qualification, each pilot must complete a specified number of landings, eight during the day and eight at night. The training involved 72 landings for the nine participating pilots.

Discussing the carrier qualifications, Major Eric Scheibe, VMA-223's executive officer said: "Being able to operate alongside the navy and understand their requirements helps us meet our own qualifications on the marine side. This way, when we transition to workups, we're already ahead in pilot qualifications."

Explaining the methodology, Gunnery Sergeant Stephen Hughson, also assigned to VMA-223, said: "This short underway provides our marines with valuable experience on the ship without the high intensity of operational activities that we will face when we set sail across the Atlantic. It allows them to move slowly and methodically, helping them understand how the ship operates and how to effectively integrate with the ship's personnel.

"One of the biggest challenges we may face is the lack of experience on both the marine aviation side and the flight deck crew. It's essential to ensure effective communication between both teams so that we can effectively work together.

"It is vital that the integration process goes smoothly so that everyone knows what their role is and how that role plays into mission success. To address any knowledge gap, we need to engage in substantial training so that our personnel are fully prepared for their responsibilities once on board."

Prior to the at-sea training, sailors assigned to *Iwo Jima*'s air department trained with VMA-223 at Marine Corps Auxiliary Landing Field Bogue near Cherry Point when the squadron was conducting practice landings on a runway marked out like an LHD flight deck.

Commenting on the training, Chief Aviation Boatswain's Mate (Handling) Jason Morris, assigned to *Iwo Jima* said: "We were able to gain invaluable training in preparation for our fixed wing certification giving us the ability to interact with our marine counterparts allowing us to operate more efficiently."

During the training, the team of sailors participated in classroom sessions where they spoke with the pilots who would later land on *Iwo Jima*'s flight deck.

Providing further insight, Chief Aviation Boatswain's Mate (Handling) Morris said: "After the classroom training, we received hands-on training and our 'blue shirts' were able to observe the procedures taken by marines in chalking and chaining the Harriers so that when we got underway, we were able to conduct the procedures ourselves ultimately leading to us certifying for flight operations."

Right: **Marines assigned to Marine Attack Squadron 231 (VMA-231) stage an AV-8B Harrier II for flight operations at Naval Air Facility El Centro, California, on February 4, 2025. VMA-231 deployed to NAF El Centro to conduct unit-level training and support marine ground units during an exercise.** USMC/Cpl David Ornelas Baeza

Below: **AV-8B Harrier II+ BuNo 165428 assigned to Marine Attack Squadron 231 (VMA-231) lands at Marine Corps Air Station Yuma, Arizona, on June 10, 2025.** USMC/LCpl Hannah Dodson

Throughout the underway period the *Iwo Jima*'s air department conducted 113 evolutions, 32 fixed wing, 59 helicopter, and 22 tiltrotor evolutions.

Regarding the air department's involvement in the training, Commander Todd Trago, USS *Iwo Jima*'s air boss, said: "They've been studying, they've been practicing, and they've been drilling day in and day out in preparation for it. They were just itching to get out on the flight deck, which speaks volumes to them because the weather conditions were freezing cold in the 30°s [-1°C] with sustained winds over 30-plus knots over the flight deck… it was impressive to see them operate and do it safely."

The USS *Iwo Jima*, with the 22nd MEU embarked was conducting COMPTUEX in the western Atlantic Ocean in July in preparation for its forthcoming deployment. An element from VMA-223 will be part of the 22nd MEU, making it the AV-8B Harrier's final at-sea deployment with the USMC.

OVERWATCH, COMMUNICATION AND **DECEPTION**

An overview of the US Marine Corps' MQ-9A Reaper fleet including its requirement, operations and leading-edge technology integrated on the aircraft.

ON FEBRUARY 3, 2025, Lieutenant General Bradford Gering, Deputy Commandant for Marine Aviation unveiled the USMC's 2025 Aviation Plan, In the section about the MQ-9 force, which included The MUX MALE programme (MUX stands for Marine Air-Ground Task Force Un-Manned Expeditionary and MALE medium-altitude high-endurance), Gering said: "The MUX MALE programme is divided into two increments. Increment I includes MQ-9A aircraft, command-and-control equipment, and operator training equipment, that last of which will be delivered Q1 FY2026. Increment II includes externally carried sensors with an IOC planned for Q1 FY2026 [October to December 2025] and an FOC for Q4 FY2030 [July to September 2030]."

Marine Unmanned Aerial Vehicle squadrons (VMUs) conduct remote split operations using beyond line-of-sight, landline, and/or satellite-based communications and two control elements, each comprising a mission control element located in the United States, and a launch and recovery element located at a location outside of the US.

Gering continued: "Under increment I, the VMUs currently operate ten MQ-9A Block 5-20 aircraft, two MQ-9A Block 5-25 aircraft, controlled by five Block 30 ground control stations [GCS]. By Q1 FY2026 [October-December 2025], the US Marine Corps will field 18 fleet aircraft, all in Block 5-25 configuration, along with 14 Block 30 GCS [seven fixed, and seven that are mobile] and six version I Airborne Network Extension payloads. VMU-1 and VMU-3 will each operate six MQ-9As, and VMX-1 will operate two aircraft."

A communications payload called the Airborne Network Extension (ANE) which enhances the MQ-9's ability to extend and relay communication signals, functions as a bridge between different networks and users, including ground forces and ships.

When Increment II achieves initial operating capability (IOC), the service expects to have three ANE(V)2 payloads, three electronic warfare support (ES) payloads and the operating infrastructure at the mission control element.

By FY2026 October the VMUs will be using a capability known as Proliferated Low Earth Orbit (pLEO) which refers to a constellation of small, affordable satellites operating in low earth orbit. The pLEO features architecture that enhances communication and surveillance and remains free of other satellite communications.

By FY2028 all VMUs will be fully equipped with MQ-9s integrated with the ES payload, followed in FY2029-2031 with a detect and avoid system, and between FY2027-2030 enhanced maritime reconnaissance payloads.

When Increment II achieves FOC, the MQ-9 fleet will have a full complement of 20 ANE(V)2s, ten ES and ten enhanced maritime reconnaissance payloads.

The MQ-9A VMU squadrons use contracted maintenance for ongoing sustainment and for the development of a standard uniform sustainment model. In FY2026, Unmanned Aerial System Maintenance Squadron 1 (UASMS-1), co-located with VMUT-2 at MCAS Cherry Point, North Carolina, will be officially activated to manage maintenance and sustainment of the MQ-9A Reaper system in the US and at overseas locations.

Once established, UASMS-1 will comprise a headquarters element and nine detachments to support two launch and recovery sites located outside the US and VMUT-2, the fleet replacement squadron. The USMC expects to establish the first maintenance detachment by Q2 FY2028.

Discussing training programs, Gering said: "US Marine Corps MQ-9A training has been supported by the US Air Force since 2018 through the Inter-service

Above: **An MQ-9A Reaper assigned to Air Test and Evaluation 24 based at Naval Air Station Patuxent River, Maryland, during the loading of the first SkyTower II pod on February 25, 2025.** Naval Air Systems Command

Training Review Organization [ITRO] agreement. Beginning in FY2025 the marine corps will establish its own training capability through the air vehicle aircrew [AVP] programme at Naval Air Station Pensacola, Florida, and VMUT-2, based at MCAS Cherry Point, North Carolina."

Concluding, Gering said: "VMUT-2 will receive four MQ-9A aircraft and three ground control stations by Q4 FY2025 [July to September 2025] to supply VMU-1 and VMU-3 with trained operators. Contract instructors will supplement the existing marine instructor cadre to sustain throughput during the training phase. The first class of student UAS aircrews were projected to begin in Q2 FY2025. Initial annual projections for aircrew and sensor operators for FY2025 is ten student crew pairs and from FY2026, 20 student crew pairs."

Born in Afghanistan

The USMC's adoption of the General Atomics Aerospace Systems Incorporated (GA-ASI) MQ-9A Reaper unmanned aerial system (UAS) was born from combat ops in Afghanistan. Combatant commanders identified the need for a system that could provide overwatch of combat ops with a persistent intelligence, surveillance, and reconnaissance capability.

An urgent operational need (UON) was issued to meet the capability gap that was impacting the ongoing operations against insurgents in Afghanistan. The USMC also used the system selected as a proof of concept for building a Group 5 UAS community, an initiative that helped inform the service about a programme it called MUX, see below. Group 5 is the classification given to a UAS based on size, weight, and capability by the Department of Defense.

In September 2018, Marine Unmanned Aerial Vehicle Squadron 1 (VMU-1) started operating MQ-9A aircraft leased from GA-ASI to fulfil the UON. The squadron based at Marine Corps Air Station Yuma, Arizona, gathered information, learned lessons, identified requirements, and developed tactics, techniques, and procedures to aid the USMC's effort for the successful acquisition and fielding of its MUX programme. MUX is the programme abbreviation for the Marine Air-Ground Task Force (MAGTF) Unmanned Aircraft System (UAS), Expeditionary (MUX) family of systems.

On March 20, 2020, US Marine Corps pilots and sensor operators assigned to VMU-1 conducted the first operational MQ-9A mission in the US Central Command's area of operation.

Crews assigned to VMU-1 took control of an MQ-9A to support marines fighting

Left: **A US Marine works on assembling an MQ-9A at Marine Corps Air Station Kaneohe Bay, Hawaii on May 10, 2023** USMC/Cpl Christian Tofteroo

in Afghanistan, with oversight provided by a GA-ASI team. The mission took place after the USMC had surpassed 7,000 hours of flight operations under a contractor-owned contractor-operated (COCO) model contract.

GA-ASI completed the transfer of two MQ-9A Reaper Block 5 aircraft to the US Marine Corps on October 15, 2021. The two aircraft had been operated since 2018 using remote split operations from Yuma, as part of a lease agreement between GA-ASI and Naval Air Systems Command. The company supported VMU-1 during the transition from operations conducted under the COCO contractor owned/contractor operated and then GOCO (Government owned contractor operated) contract models, between 2020 and 2021.

After transitioning from COCO to GOCO aircraft, VMU-1 undertook the USMC's first MQ-9A flight at Marine Corps Aircraft Station Yuma, Arizona, on August 30, 2021. The flight culminated three years of training, establishing safety and operational planning, and contractor maintenance, to ensure adherence to USN and USMC aviation policies.

Major Keenan Chirhart, VMU-1's then executive officer said: "VMU-1 is laying the groundwork for future squadrons to execute similar missions within the US Indo-Pacific Command."

The transition from COCO to GOCO enabled VMU-1 to fly and operate a forward-deployed MQ-9A to undertake missions that involved gathering data in highly contested areas from a remote location, Yuma, while the MQ-9 aircraft was physically located in another combatant commander's area of operation.

The two aircraft accrued over 12,000 flight hours supporting operations in the US Central Command (CENTCOM) area of responsibility (AOR) and in support of the MUX programme, which by now had been defined with 20 Block 5 MQ-9A aircraft. A Block 5 MQ-9A has an endurance of over 26 hours, flies at up to 220kts airspeed, can operate at up to 45,000ft altitude, with a 3,850lb payload capacity that includes 3,000lb of external stores.

Despite VMU-1's trailblazing efforts with the MQ-9A. VMU-3 based at Marine Corps Base Kaneohe, Hawaii, was the first VMU to achieve initial operational capability with the MQ-9A platform in August 2023.

On May 27, 2022, GA-ASI was awarded a contract for eight MQ-9A Extended

Below: **US Marines work on an MQ-9A's Honeywell TPE331 engine at Marine Corps Air Station Kaneohe Bay, Hawaii.** USMC/Cpl Christian Tofteroo

Above: An MQ-9A assigned to Marine Unmanned Aerial Vehicle Squadron 3 completes the pre-flight checklist for the first satellite communications launch and recovery mission at Marine Corps Air Station Kaneohe Bay, Hawaii, on June 20, 2024. USMC/ Cpl Joseph Abreu

Range (ER) unmanned aircraft systems as part of the ARES (Agile Reaper Enterprise Solution) contract: the first increment of new aircraft procured under the MUX programme.

On November 10, 2022, GA-ASI flew the first production MQ-9A configured for multi-domain operations. Dubbed the Block 5-25 M2DO, the upgraded aircraft includes features to enable future integration and fielding of open mission systems, new sensors, improved power distribution and redundancy, GPS improvements, radar altimeters, nose wheel steering, and angle of attack sensor system improvements.

GA-ASI delivered the first two new-build MQ-9A ER aircraft to Naval Air Systems Command on April 19, 2023. These two aircraft were the first of the eight ordered in 2022 for the MUX programme.

Weapons and Tactics Instruction

Each year, Marine Aviation Weapons and Tactics Squadron 1 (MAWTS-1) based at Yuma provides standardised advanced tactical training and certification of weapon officer. The squadron runs two seven-week weapons and tactics instructor (WTI) courses each year. The WTI programme plays a crucial role in developing and employing the latest tactics over land and in maritime environment.

Dubbed WTI 1-24, the first course of FY2024, which finished on October 29, 2023, involved Block 5 MQ-9A operations. Marine aviators were trained using one of the two MQ-9s leased from GA-ASI, who, after graduation, were posted to fleet VMU squadrons to serve as weapons officers and the resident expert in the employment of the Block 5 MQ-9A. Their WTI training was rated as a critical part of the MUX programme for meeting full operational capability.

Night Owls

Marine Unmanned Aerial Vehicle Training Squadron 2 (VMUT-2) 'Night Owls', a component squadron of the 2nd Marine Aircraft Wing based at Marine Corps Air Station Cherry Point, began assembling its first MQ-9A Reaper on April 10, 2024. Many of the parts were delivered to VMUT-2 from GA-ASI on March 18, 2024, one of eight MQ-9A ER aircraft ordered in November 2022.

The training squadron is re-equipping with the Reaper as part of a transition by all VMU squadrons from the legacy RQ-21A Blackjack in accordance with the USMC' Force Design initiatives.

On November 21, 2024, VMUT-2) conducted its first MQ-9A Reaper flight at MCAS Cherry Point. The squadron started its transition from the RQ-21A Blackjack as the USMC MQ-9A fleet replacement squadron in July 2023. Its primary role is to train USMC MQ-9 pilots and sensor operators in their respective military occupational specialties, At the time of the first flight, VMUT-2 expected to receive its first class of student MQ-9 pilots and sensor operators in the spring of 2025.

Commenting on the first flight, Lieutenant Colonel Jonathan Boersma, VMUT-2's commanding officer said: "This achievement is more than a technical success – it represents a bold step forward in the future of unmanned aerial systems within the US Marine Corps. Our instructors here get to shape the next generation of UAS operators, instilling in them the skills and standards required to support the fleet and uphold the proud traditions of marine aviation."

SkyTower and T-SOAR

When the seven-week WTI 2-24 course finished at Yuma on April 20, 2024, it concluded participation of the SkyTower I pod, a USMC-specific payload for the MQ-9A.

SkyTower I provides a MAGTF with extended airborne communication capabilities in various waveforms including a commercial-quality WiFi network, and a relay/repeater function connecting geographically disconnected teams.

In early June 2024, the US Naval Institute posted a story about USMC MQ-9A Reapers operating from Basa Air Base in the Philippines.

According to the online report, USMC unmanned aerial vehicles started operating from Basa Air Base in the spring of 2024 at the request of the Government of the Philippines to support intelligence sharing efforts between US Indo-Pacific Command and the Armed Forces of the Philippines.

A spokesperson for Camp Pendleton, California-based I Marine Expeditionary Force, told *US Naval Institute* news: "The marine corps will employ unarmed MQ-9As to provide reconnaissance and surveillance in support of the development of intelligence sharing between the US and our Philippine allies and in accordance with Philippine national laws, rules, and regulations. The drones are in the Philippines on a rotational basis, which is permitted under the 2014 Enhanced Defense Cooperation Agreement."

This was the first foreign deployment for USMC MQ-9s since they achieved IOC capability in the summer of 2023 with VMU-3. The aircraft are providing maritime domain awareness and overwatch of the Second Thomas Shoal, a submerged reef in the South China Sea.

Speaking at the Brooking Institution on July 2, 2024, USMC commandant General Eric Smith discussed an electronic warfare pod carried by the MQ-9. He said: "It's called a T-SOAR pod and can mimic things that it detects, turn it around and send it back, so it becomes a black hole… It has the ability to somewhat disappear off an enemy radar."

GA-ASI product data says the SOAR (Scalable Open Architecture Reconnaissance) pod provides long-range detection, identification, and location of radar and communication signals of interest. SOAR enables MQ-9 or other aircraft operators to provide standoff surveillance – seeing threats before threats can see the aircraft – and communicate actionable intelligence.

By leveraging US government technology in strategic ISR (intelligence, surveillance, and reconnaissance) systems, the T-SOAR system provides a low-cost, widely deployable capability for a variety of national security council and combatant command signals intelligence collection objectives. T-SOAR provides real time collection, onboard storage for post-mission analysis, and enables multi-intelligence target identification and tracking in real time. A T-SOAR pod houses L3Harris full-band signals intelligence systems housed inside a wing-mounted pod which weighs over 600lb and measures 125(L) x 29(D) x 25(W)ins.

An operational evaluation (OPEVAL) of the T-SOAR system conducted between 3Q FY2020 through 1Q FY2021 validated the pod's ability to conduct long-range surveillance from a persistent/low-cost unmanned aircraft system, supported artificial intelligence and machine learning, and included missions via remote split operations that allowed CONUS-based aircrews to operate and control the aircraft and payload flying overseas.

T-SOAR features open architecture with commercial-off-the-shelf/government-off-the-shelf standards, enables collaborative operations, cross-cueing to on-board sensors, real-time remote operations, and secure mission data storage.

SATCOM Launch and Recovery

On June 20, 2024, VMU-3 successfully conducted a satellite communications (SATCOM) launch and recovery (SLR) with an MQ-9A. It was the first ever SLR mission involving USMC aviators operating a USMC aircraft at a Marine Corps Air Station.

Traditionally, launch and recovery elements are tethered to cumbersome line-of-sight (LOS) command and control equipment, necessitating specialised aviators and large transport aircraft to begin operations at established airfields.

Below: **An MQ-9A assigned to Marine Unmanned Aerial Vehicle Squadron 3 taxis at Marine Corps Air Station Kaneohe Bay, Hawaii, June 20, 2024. The aircraft is loaded with a SkyTower II pod on its port side under wing station and a T-SOAR pod on the starboard side.** USMC/Cpl Joseph Abreu

Left: **An MQ-9A Reaper assigned to Marine Unmanned Aerial Vehicle Squadron 1 disassembled inside a Reaper box, officially called a shipping and storage container, at Marine Corps Air Station Yuma, Arizona.** USMC/LCpl Jade Venegas

By comparison, SLR uses current satellite-based infrastructure, to enable US Marines to overcome the constraint of LOS command and control equipment, increase the operational flexibility of a forward deployed MQ-9A and increased the number of available airfields from where VMU-3 can operate.

The successful SLR demonstration emphasises the squadrons' pivotal role in advancing USMC capabilities in reconnaissance, surveillance, and target acquisition missions across the Indo-Pacific region. By minimising the number of logistical constraints and enabling operations from short airfields over vast distances, SLR supports the hub-and-spoke concept of operations: conducting flights from a central hub to multiple smaller destinations, known as spokes, thereby increasing the flexibility required for expeditionary operations: a crucial capability for maintaining a forward presence that's sustainable and survivable.

According to the USMC, SLR is a strategic move to keep MQ-9A operations expeditionary and adaptable.

Okinawa Ops

Six USMC MQ-9A Reaper aircraft were airlifted to Kadena Air Base in Okinawa in mid-August 2024 for a 12-month deployment. A USMC photo showed the MQ-9s being unloaded from a USAF C-17 on August 13.

The aircraft were flying ISR missions around the southwest region of Japan. Details of the deployment were released by Japan's Ministry of Defense following a meeting by the Japan-US Security Consultative Committee in Tokyo on July 28. The aircraft were tasked to provide surveillance of Chinese and North Korean seaborne activity in the region. The Reapers were assigned to and operated by VMU-3. During its participation in Exercise RIMPAC in July 2024, VMU-3 conducted multi-intelligence reconnaissance in support of live-fire exercises, naval surface escort missions, photo exercises, and operating as the command-and-control node for an amphibious landing in Hawaii.

SkyTower II

Personnel assigned to Air Test and Evaluation 24 (UX-24) based at Naval Air Station Patuxent River, Maryland, loaded the first SkyTower II pod onto an MQ-9A aircraft on February 25, 2025. Initial power-on checks were conducted as the first step of integrating the pod onto an MQ-9A Reaper.

Commenting in a Naval Air Systems Command press release, Captain Dennis Monagle, Multi-Mission Tactical UAS programme manager said: "Over the past two years, we've partnered with GALT Aerospace, a small business vendor, to rapidly develop this unique capability… With robust system and integration

MQ-9A REAPER SPECIFICATIONS

Wingspan	66ft
Length	36ft
Powerplant	Honeywell TPE331-10
Max gross take-off weight	10,500lb
Fuel capacity	3,900lb
Internal payload capacity	850lb
External payload	3,000lb
Hard points	Six, all underwing
Payloads	MTS-B EO/IR, Lynx multi-mode radar, multi-mode maritime radar, automated identification system, and communications relay
Power	11.0kW/45.0 kVA (Block 5)
Max altitude	50,000ft
Max endurance	27 hours
Max radius	2,250nm
Max airspeed	240kts
Cruise speed	166kts

Notes: A Block 5 MQ-9A provides multi-sensor surveillance and reconnaissance; data gateway and relay capabilities via an aerial layer network; and enables or can conduct the detection and engagement of targets during expeditionary, joint, and combined operations. An MQ-9A can also undertake maritime domain awareness, provide airborne early warning and electronic support, and extend the range of an airborne network.

testing now underway, we remain on track to achieve initial operating capability this year [2025]."

According to GALT Aerospace, SkyTower II is a podded airborne network extension and gateway that provides cross-domain communications and data relay capability. When configured with a SkyTower II pod, an MQ-9 functions as a critical link between marine corps aviation and ground combat elements, providing enhanced multidomain situational awareness and command-and-control.

GALT aerospace lists SkyTower II with the following capabilities: secure dissemination of mission critical data across a gateway-connected network; provision of numerous resilient paths for data exchange; and provision of mission-critical data exchanges within denied or contested environments.

UX-24 also completed a fit check of the MQ-9 in the anechoic chamber at Patuxent River in late February. The team conducted several tests and hoisted the aircraft for the first time as a risk reduction event

Below: **A Reaper box being unloaded from a KC-130J Hercules at Marine Corps Air Station Miramar, California. Disassembly, transport, and reassembly of the aircraft between Yuma and Miramar served as a proof of concept for the Reaper's rapid, expeditionary deployment capacity.** USMC/ Sgt Rachaelanne Woodward

Above: **The first MQ-9A Reaper assigned to the USMC at an undisclosed location in the US Central Command area of responsibility.** USMC

for electromagnetic compatibility (EMC) testing, a process that verifies the aircraft's subsystems function without interfering with each other.

NAVAIR's Electromagnetic Environmental Effects (E3) division and the Electromagnetic Compatibility (EMC) branch, provide E3 systems engineering expertise and test and evaluation of all naval aviation aircraft, weapon, and ground support systems and their functionality within naval aviation's unique operational electromagnetic environment. Testing is undertaken to verify a system against electromagnetic interference, electromagnetic vulnerability, and electromagnetic pulses.

UX-24 is continuing to test the SkyTower II and expects to complete testing in time to release the system to VMU-3 for deployment in 2026.

During a presentation at the modern-day marine conference in April 2025, Lieutenant Colonel Eric Duchene spoke about several new systems for the MQ-9A Reaper. These included the SkyTower II airborne network extension system, pods for electronic warfare and maritime domain awareness, a detect-and-avoid system, satellite command and control, and smart sensors.

Duchene said: "That provides AI-enabled [by high-power computer processing] persistent presence in the battlespace. We're looking to field advanced

Right: **This photo of a US Marine Corps MQ-9A shows the side elevation of the SkyTower II pod loaded on the under-wing pylon and the markings including the MARINES title, bureau number and squadron tail code.** USMC

capabilities that allow us to find, fix and track our targets of interest, and then be able to disseminate that to the MAGTF and the joint force.

"Fielding this capability will be critical to reducing the pilot and sensor operator workload inside the battlespace to find, fix, track and target targets of interest. What this does… with sensor autonomy is it minimises the time by automating what would normally be a manual three-ball collect on a target, of trying to find and then progressively get closer and closer to the target, refine what you're seeing,

identify it. We're looking to lessen that workload to then free up the operator to do more advanced things like develop a track, and then be able to employ that and it throughout the joint force."

He continued: "A bundled release of Sky Tower II electronic warfare payloads and the smart sensor system are slated for [service introduction] the last quarter of this calendar year."

To meet the needs of marines, the service wants to develop a pipeline to modify artificial intelligence and machine learning tools. Commenting, Duchene said: "When we collect data, we can rapidly retrain, and put out new models. As an operator, eventually you'll be able to take a new model, determine that the algorithm doesn't work, and maybe in real-time get it fixed, and then re-upload it, so tweaking your algorithm while you're flying and getting a better find, fix and track capability."

Fused Data in WTI

During WTI course 2-25 staged in March and April, personnel assigned to MAWTS-1 and VMX-1, working with engineers from GA-ASI and General Atomics Integrated Intelligence, successfully integrated the advanced Optix software –developed by GA-i3 – into the USMC common intelligence picture during the course.

MQ-9A flight operations took place at Yuma, Arizona, and the USMC's only expeditionary runway in the United States known as the SELF (Strategic Expeditionary Landing Field) located at Marine Corps Air Ground Combat Center Twentynine Palms in California. Using an MQ-9 loaded with the advanced Optix software enabled operators to access fused data for real-time situational awareness, a shared operational picture, and an enhanced decision-making process across the battlespace —tools that are critical for the training of WTI students.

Above: **A US Marine Corps MQ-9A Reaper loaded with a SkyTower II pod.** USMC

Below: **Air Test and Evaluation 24 completed a fit check of the MQ-9 in the anechoic chamber at Patuxent River in late February 2025.** Naval Air Systems Command

SUBSCRIBE TODAY
TO YOUR FAVOURITE MAGAZINE!
BAD TO THE BONE INSIDE DYESS AFB'S B-1 FORCE
COMBAT AIRCRAFT
JOURNAL
AMERICA'S BEST SELLING MILITARY AVIATION MAGAZINE
TANK KILLERS
Combat marks the 50th anniversary of the Apache
READY TO FIGHT CHINA
How Taiwan will fight off invasion
LAST
TO
How the
Iran's
DRAGON LADY
HITS 70 Celebrating seven decades of U-2 ops
SCAN ME
Combat Aircraft Journal
is renowned for being America's best selling military aviation magazine.
SIMPLY SCAN THE QR CODE OF YOUR FAVOURITE MAGAZINE AND SUBSCRIBE TODAY!
Order today from our online shop
shop.keypublishing.com
Call +44 (0)1780 480404 (Mon to Fri 9am - 5.30pm GMT)

Avove: A KC-130J Super Hercules assigned to Marine Aerial Refueler Transport Squadron 152 conducts a touch-and-go on an assault landing zone at Joint Base Elmendorf-Richardson, Alaska, during exercise Red-Flag Alaska. USMC/ LCpl Cecilia Campbell

Gering said: "The 2025 Aviation Plan demonstrates our resolute dedication to maintaining operational superiority and ensuring we are always ready to project force, wherever and whenever needed."

Strategy

Outlining the strategy behind Project Eagle, Gering said: "We will deliver a lethal, effective, and survivable capability to enable naval and joint campaigning in all domains. While operating from austere, distributed locations and across extended distances, we will be minimally sustained, fully networked, and entirely interoperable with the Joint Force and America's allies and partners. In line with Force Design (a restructuring initiative introduced by General David Berger in March 2020 aimed at modernising the Marine Corps' combat capabilities to address future near-peer adversary conflicts), we will continue

to cultivate an integrated total force, where reserve component marines and units from the 4th Marine Aircraft Wing (MAW) provide augmentation, reinforcement, and sustainment to the active component across all aviation functions.

"Our efforts are guided by the following priorities: support the Marine Air-Ground Task Force [MAGTF] via the functions of marine aviation; ensure detailed collaboration and interoperability with the Joint Force; and support broader allied force and partner nation efforts of interoperability.

"Project Eagle's objective [over the next three Future Years Defense Programs or FYDPs] is to achieve a framework that enables the US Marine Corps to adjust the track of the current planning, programming, budgeting, and execution assessment [PPBEA] process."

The FYDP is a projection of the forces, resources, and programs required to support Department of Defense (DOD)

operations. The revised approach outlined by Gering is intended to determine the capabilities and technological innovations required to exceed the projection of a single FYDP and enable the USMC to plan beyond the current FYDP and PPBEA process.

Gering used the term 'lines of effort' to refer to the work undertaken to achieve four major goals of Project Eagle.

1. Focus on the viability of the new DAO and DCAO concepts of operation which are meant to support Distributed Maritime Operations (DMO), Expeditionary Advanced Base Operations (EABO), Stand-in Force (SIF), and broader force modernisation efforts, all designed to drive marine aviation strategy, doctrine, and acquisitions."

2. Develop a modernised functional framework for marine aviation necessary for MAGTF planners to uses when preparing for a maritime

campaign. According to Gering, the USMC will codify aviation ground support as a doctrinal function of marine aviation in support of the MAGTF and Joint Force.

3. Create a data centric and data enabled organisation so marine aviation can maintain a competitive advantage in future conflicts and meet the current mission requirements. Gering said this evolution will allow marine aviation to use artificial intelligence and machine learning, and require investment in infrastructure, personnel, and training.

4. Address specific priorities and allocation of resources and funding across the next three FYDPs and beyond. Gering highlighted future unmanned platforms that support logistics as one example.

Summing up, Gering said: "Project Eagle is my vision for force transformation and ensures marine aviation provides the cutting-edge advantage to the naval force that supports the MAGTF and the Joint Force."

Aviation Readiness

Providing insight to aviation readiness, the capability of a squadron to perform assigned missions and tasks effectively and efficiently, Gering said: "Marine aviation is tasked with maintaining high operational readiness to respond to crisis today, while ensuring our multiple communities in transition maintain their momentum to fight tomorrow. To sustain a lethal capability ready to respond to crisis, marine aviation will focus on readiness, manpower, and aviation enablers.

"Operational readiness is my number one priority. The readiness of marine aviation is fundamentally linked to its ability to respond to crises swiftly and effectively. Our readiness strategy encompasses several key elements designed to address these needs. First and foremost, it includes robust efforts to maintain our current aircraft. This involves continued investment in sustainment programs to ensure our aircraft, aircrew, and maintainers are ready to fight tonight. Such programs are critical for managing the operational demands placed on the entire fleet and ensure their reliability. By sufficiently funding our sustainment and readiness accounts, along with our flight hour programme we will ensure we have the necessary mission capable aircraft on our flight lines, and our aircrew have the appropriate number of reps and sets in training.

"Simultaneously, we are focused on modernising our fleet. The goal is to ensure that our new platforms and systems can seamlessly integrate

Below: **A KC-130J Super Hercules stages for pre-flight checks during VMGR-152's participation in Talisman Sabre 25 in the Northern Territory, Australia, on July 10, 2025.** USMC/ Cpl Chloe Johnson

into the MAGTF without disrupting current capabilities. We have worked with the Fleet Marine Force (FMF) and our various programme offices to identify potential risks associated with transitioning from legacy to new platforms and systems."

Aviation Sustainment

Sustaining aircraft, helicopters and tiltrotors assigned to USMC squadrons is an ongoing challenge, made ever more so in the face of contested, higher threat environments.

Addressing the challenges presented by sustainment, Gering said: "Our traditional aviation sustainment methods, while effective in the past, are no longer sufficient to meet the challenges operating in current and future contested environments. To overcome these challenges, we need to work together with key stakeholders, including type-model-series leads, programme offices, and logistics teams. Through a collaborative approach, marine aviation will identify and prioritise sustainment solutions, focusing on three lines of effort that will drive change and ensure the sustainment of our ready force.

1. Focus on a demand-based, bottom-up strategy that is responsive to fleet readiness needs. Squadrons conducting sustainment activities will function as readiness engines and generate the touch-time needed to achieve materiel condition improvements.
2. Pursue sustainment solutions that are effective in DAO. Gering highlighted the importance of evaluating all maintenance activities needed to maintain a weapon system throughout its lifespan to determine how to sustain distributed operations involving small units spread across a large area of operations undertaking independent tactical ops. This will require a thorough examination and refinement of the policies governing current maintenance practices, including:
   - Redesigning support equipment where required, to enhance efficiency, safety, and effectiveness.
   - Modernising training systems to ensure personnel possess cross-functional competencies and the required skills to use emerging technologies.
   - Accelerating the development and implementation of, for example, additive manufacturing and digital twin modelling, to improve supply chain resilience and reduce lead times.
   - Fostering a culture of innovation and experimentation within the aviation sustainment community to drive the adoption of best practices and emerging technologies.
3. Optimise current sustainment efforts and reduce variability in aircraft and equipment readiness by pursuing key initiatives to ensure sustainable logistics; deliver effective tooling and equipment to the flightline; enable effective maintenance management and flight operations scheduling to achieve flight hour goals and readiness; optimise all aviation sustainment information systems; improve maintenance capacity by standardising leadership engagement; and by expanding the Marine Corps' partnership with industry to offer advanced maintenance training.

Improving Readiness

Citing the ability to fight tonight and current readiness of marine aviation as his priorities, Gering said: "The Naval Aviation Enterprise [NAE] exists for naval aviation stakeholders to share information, identify challenges, and remove barriers to readiness. NAE's framework facilitates the collaboration, transparency, engagement, and process improvement for the NAE's various naval stakeholders. The process used by the Navy Sustainment System for Aviation [NSS-A] supports pillars that are designed to transform our

Below: An AH-1Z Viper assigned to Marine Light Attack Helicopter Squadron 367 during Service Level Training Exercise 4-25 at Marine Corps Air-Ground Combat Center, Twentynine Palms, on August 11, 2025. USMC/ LCpl Seferino Gamez

aviation sustainment capabilities. These include reforming our supply chain, engineering, and fleet readiness centres to improve governance, accountability, and organisation; establishing a Maintenance Operations Center [MOC] to better manage aircraft-on-ground situations; and implementing maintenance management at organisational level to streamline maintenance processes. While we initially stepped back from the MOC concept in 2023, several teams recognised its benefits. We are now piloting the KC-130J MOC to assess its effectiveness before deciding whether to expand it to other type-model-series [TMS]."

Outlining his thinking about the modernisation of commodities used for maintaining aircraft, helicopters and tiltrotors, Gering highlighted the need for successful modernisation, integration, and performance of commodity enablers, those things that enable the efficient movement, storage, or exchange of commodities required by marine aviation, as key for optimising current sustainment efforts to reduce variability in aircraft and equipment readiness.

By focussing on key areas, such as aviation supply packages, aviation logistics support ships, avionics repair capabilities, and ordnance, marine aviation will be able to create sustainment strategies based on data.

Aviation Supply Packages

Gering said the Marine Aviation Logistics Support Program (MALSP) must undergo a significant modernisation to successfully support distributed aviation operations. Supply packages must be redesigned to provide sufficient depth to sustain a highly dynamic, nodal web of aircraft and support sites which will require changing the traditional aggregation-based approach. Consequently, the existing Primary Aircraft Authorised-based modelling must be revised to optimise for decentralised operations, rather than the current cost-wise return on investment model. This will enable the support of a distributed lay down of aircraft, helicopters, and tiltrotors for extended durations.

By transitioning the aviation supply process, the marine aviation is reviewing its support packages and updating its stock levels to reflect the latest configuration and failure rates.

Marine aviation is also reviewing the requirement for one afloat spares package (ASP) per deployment site and exploring an option to share risk with industry in physically rebuilding surge ASP(s) within an operational window. According to Gering, this has the potential to reduce costs and improve the ability to respond to operational needs. Marine aviation is also evaluating spares packages for the F-35 to ensure effective support of F-35B and F-35C aircraft.

Above: **An AH-1Z assigned to Marine Light Helicopter Attack Squadron 775 conducts close air support at Exercise Northern Strike 25-2, at Camp Grayling, Michigan, on August 10, 2025. Northern Strike is a National Guard Bureau-sponsored, multi component, multinational exercise designed to build readiness and enhance interoperability with allied forces.** US Army/Sgt Dana Vermilye

Aviation Logistics Support Ships

Both US Navy (USN) aviation logistics support vessels (SS *Wright* T-AVB 3 and SS *Curtis* T-AVN 4) are planned for retirement in 2030 and 2033. Consequently, the USMC will experience a critical shortfall if replacements are not pursued. Gering said marine aviation requires a standing capability to conduct afloat aviation sustainment activities to support EABO and DAO. Marine aviation is pursuing a replacement, T-AVB(Next), that should offer a stand-in force (a small, lethal, and mobile force operating as a forward-deployed, persistent presence to deter adversaries and disrupt their operations) the following capabilities:

- Sea-based mobility and cargo handling.
- Intermediate maintenance activities to reduce deployment and sustainment timelines.
- Flexibility to support both aviation and ground maintenance operations.
- Scalable, modular, and flexible capacity to accommodate up to 400 deployable maintenance facilities.
- Ability to self-load at multiple access points, including lift-on/lift-off (LOLO) cranes and roll-on/roll-off (RO-RO) ramps.
- Day and night flight deck operations and aircraft refuelling capability.
- Vertical and connected replenishment from combat logistic fleet vessels.

Avionics Repair Capabilities

Avionics are critical to all aircraft so the ability to undertake repairs of avionics is crucial for which marine aviation continues to use Automatic Test Equipment (ATE), but the system is nearing the end of its service life.

Its replacement is called the electronic Consolidated Automated Support System (eCASS) which is already in transition at USN shore bases and aboard CVN and L-Class ships. The fleet will begin to receive the eCASS benches beginning in FY2025 in support of the F-35 intermediate-level maintenance requirement, but additional funding is required to upgrade the ageing test benches across the various aircraft, helicopter, and tiltrotor platforms.

Ordnance

Discussing air-to-air and air-to-ground ordnance used by marine aviation squadrons, Gering said optimising a balance between the sustainment of current operations and the modernisation of marine aviation's ordnance capabilities is crucial and requires cross-training and collaboration within marine aviation; interoperability with the Joint Force; and interoperability with partner nations to support combined ops and Joint Force readiness.

Outlining the requirements, Gering said: "As weapon systems become more advanced and costly, hands-on training with live ordnance is becoming limited. To address this limitation, we are changing the training for the aviation ordnance community by increasing availability of inert training munitions for hands-on experience and developing virtual trainers to maintain proficiency. We're also enhancing our career progression courses, expeditionary training, and initial accession training.

To support distributed operations, the current aviation weapons support equipment (AWSE) posture needs to be functional and practical. To close the gap, marine aviation is developing more efficient, transportable, and expeditionary equipment. It is also considering the use of consumable equipment to reduce the logistics burdens, and is partnering with the Joint Force to enhance interoperability and reduce redundancy.

Gering also outlined his thinking about the management of weapons inventories faced with the reality that logistics systems will be contested in any future conflict. Analysis of requirements, prepositioning opportunities, and logistical considerations to optimise the management of strategic stockpiles

Above: **An F-35B assigned to Marine Fighter Attack Squadron 242, 31st Marine Expeditionary Unit, takes-off during flight operations aboard the amphibious assault ship USS *America*, in the Philippine Sea, on August 10, 2025.** USMC/LCpl Gerardo Mendez

is underway. One key enabler is the modernisation of the ageing ammunition accounting system to improve fidelity of inventory reporting, ammunition transacting, and data analytics.

Gering summarised the Marine Aviation Sustainment Plan by listing the three key areas required to enhance overall readiness in support of the MAGTF.

1. Implement a bottom-up approach to sustainment that responds to squadron, group, and wing needs, the so-called demand-based sustainment model.
2. Pursue sustainment solutions that enable effective distributed aviation operations.
3. Reduce variability in aircraft and equipment readiness by optimising current sustainment efforts.

Aircraft, Helicopters and Tiltrotors in Marine Aviation

Marine aviation's primary role is to maintain a lethal and responsive Aviation Combat Element (ACE) to support the MAGTF and Joint Force. Currently, marine aviation is part-way through the transition to an all-F-35 tactical aircraft (TACAIR) fleet and is modernising all other aspects of the ACE.

Gering's plan included details of the transition plan for each classification of aircraft: fixed wing aircraft tactical air; tiltrotor; rotary wing aircraft heavy-lift; light attack; and unmanned.

Above: **Logistics specialists perform external lifts at Naval Air Station Key West, Florida, on July 23, 2025, during joint training with the US Army, US Navy, and US Customs and Border Protection to refine humanitarian assistance and disaster relief capabilities while also refining the CH-53K King Stallion's ability to support distributed aviation operations in a joint environment.** USMC/Cpl Mya Seymour

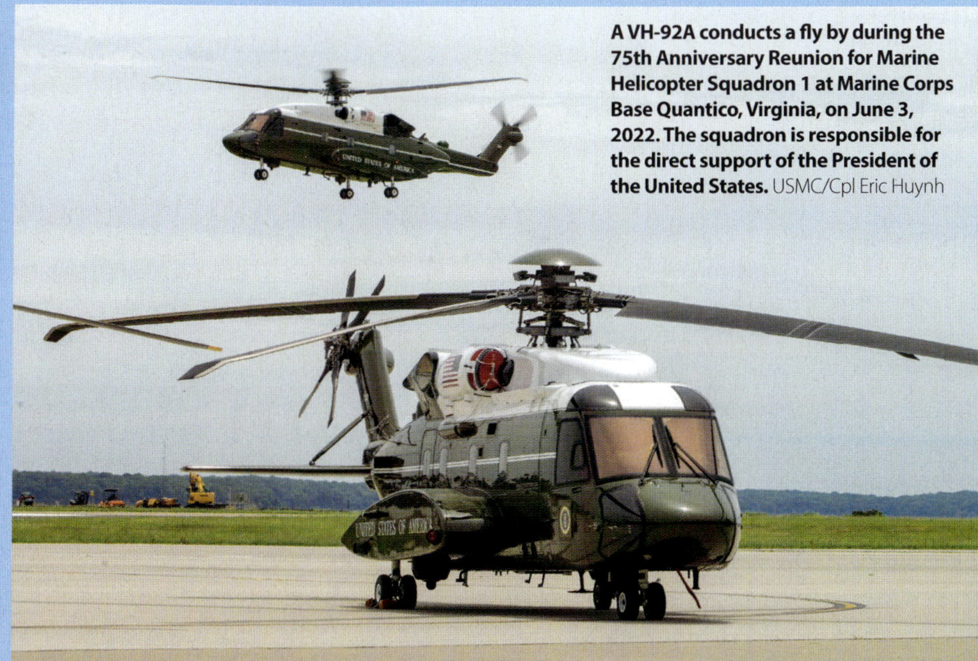

A VH-92A conducts a fly by during the 75th Anniversary Reunion for Marine Helicopter Squadron 1 at Marine Corps Base Quantico, Virginia, on June 3, 2022. The squadron is responsible for the direct support of the President of the United States. USMC/Cpl Eric Huynh

F-35 Lightning I

Marine aviation is the only US armed service that operates two versions of the F-35 Lightning II: the F-35B STOVL variant and the F-35C carrier variant. The F-35B is deployed as an element of a Marine Expeditionary Unit embarked aboard an L-class ships, the F-35C is deployed as part of a Carrier Air Wing embarked aboard a CVN carrier. Marine aviation also deploys both variants to land bases in expeditionary taskings.

By the end of 2025, 183 F-35B and 52 F-35C aircraft will have been delivered to the USMC. Those aircraft are assigned to developmental and operational test squadrons, two F-35B fleet replacement squadrons, one based at Beaufort, South Carolina and one based at Miramar, California, an F-35C FRS detachment at NAS Lemoore, California, and 11 fleet squadrons.

Gering said the programme of record (the formally approved and funded acquisition programme comprising 420 F-35 aircraft) has not changed since its inception, but its composition has changed to reflect an increase in the number of F-35C squadrons. As per the TACAIR transition plan, Marine Fighter Attack Squadron 232 (VMFA-232), VMFA-323, VMFA-112, and VMFA-134 will now transition from the F/A-18C Hornet to the F-35C. Consequently, the programme of record now comprises 280 F-35Bs and 140 F-35Cs which will equip 20 squadrons, 12 equipped with F-35Bs, and eight with F-35Cs.

All F-35 fleet squadrons currently have ten aircraft assigned. These are known as Primary Aircraft Authorisation (PAA) squadrons, which are tasked to deploy as a squadron in support of a Marine Expeditionary Unit (MEU) or a Carrier Air Wing (CVW).

In FY2024, the two F-35B squadrons based at Iwakuni, Japan, VMFA-121 and VMFA-242, were reorganised as 12 PAA squadrons. After detailed analysis, marine aviation approved a plan to increase all fleet F-35 squadrons to 12 PAA. This is now reflected in the TACAIR transition plan.

To support the increase to 12 PAA per squadron, each squadron will undergo a change to the number of marines assigned and a realignment that seeks to fill gaps in certain military occupational specialties (MOS) within the maintenance department. Each squadron's manning will increase by two pilots and 25 maintainers, with a specific focus on corrosion control.

Once the transition plan is complete, changes to manning will start in FY2028 and additional aircraft will be assigned in FY2030.

In terms of the current F-35 force posture, the type supports all deployments by the 31st MEU based in Okinawa, Japan and all MEU deployments previously supported by AV-8B Harrier VMA squadrons assigned to Marine Air Group 11 based at Yuma, Arizona. The F-35 also supports the Tactical Aviation Integration (TAI) mission, previously supported by F/A-18, which aims to combine the fixed-wing tactical aviation aircraft of both the USN and the USMC into a more unified force. As the F-35 transition continues, the type will ultimately support all Marine Air Group 14, based at Cherry Point, North Carolina MEU and Unit Deployment Program (UDP) obligations.

As part of the TAI mission, the first F-35C unit, VMFA-314 continues to operate as part of CVW-9, to be followed by VMFA-311 based at Miramar and VMFA-251 based at Cherry Point.

As the F-35 programme continues to go through upgrades and modernisation, aircraft upgraded to Technology Refresh 3 (TR-3) configuration (the foundation of future Block 4 aircraft) are being delivered to VMFA-533 at Beaufort and VMFA-251 at Cherry Point.

Modernisation initiatives include greater computational power and memory capacity, the APG-85 radar, multi-ship IRST (Infrared Search and Track), countermeasure updates, modernised electronic warfare (EW), and the next generation distributed aperture system (NG-DAS).

Below: An AH-1Z Viper assigned to Marine Light Attack Helicopter Squadron 367 during a forward arming and refuelling point event as part of Service Level Training Exercise 4-25 at Marine Corps Air Ground Combat Center, Twentynine Palms, on August 6, 2025. USMC/LCpl Enge You

Fielding of Operational Flight Program 30P08 software will enable the GBU-53/B precision strike weapon to be introduced to the fleet.

The following weapons continue to be developed for integration on the F-35 aircraft: the AGM-88G Advanced Anti-Radiation Guided Missile-Extended Range (AARGM-ER), AGM-158B Joint Air-to-Surface Standoff Missile – Extended Range (JASSM-ER) and AGM-158C Long-Range Anti-Ship Missile (LRASM), AIM-9X Block II+ Sidewinder missile, the capability to carry six AIM-120 AMRAAM missiles in an F-35C weapons bay, GBU-38 (500lb Joint Direct Attack Munition), GBU-54 (500lb Laser Joint Direct Attack Munition) will increase capability and provide enhanced lethal capabilities to the F-35.

F/A-18 Hornet

Today, the F/A-18 Hornet provides maritime strike and air interdiction capability to combatant commanders. A modernisation programme to increase survivability and lethality against both air and surface threats should enable the Hornet to continue conducting its assigned mission essential tasks (METs). According to Gering the Hornet's relevance and capacity remains a critical function of the Marine Corps' TACAIR transition plan.

Until the end of FY2025, Fleet Marine Force will maintain four active and one reserve squadron of F/A-18s using a fleet of 161 aircraft.

Structure requirements remain in place until the end of FY2029.

In FY2024, new F/A-18 aircrew training shifted to the Fleet Replacement Detachment (FRD) within the Miramar-based VMFA-323 with the assistance of contract maintenance. Key to sustaining the required number of F/A-18 aircrew is maintaining a healthy production of new pilots by the FRD, and by retaining experienced maintainers throughout the transition until the type's sundown.

One major upgrade involves installation of the APG-79(V)4 active electronically scanned array (AESA) radar, the first of which was delivered in FY2022. Coupled with the APG-79(V)4 radar, a new electronic warfare suite, the pursuit of net-enabled and extended range weapons, and beyond-line-of-sight (BLOS) communications, should maintain the Hornet's lethality and survivability against near-peer adversaries.

KC-130J Hercules

Continuously deployed since 2005, KC-130J-equipped Marine Aerial Refueler Transport Squadron (VMGR) detachments support Crisis Response-Africa, operations in Europe, the Middle East, and South America.

Activation of VMGR-153 at Marine Corps Air Station Kaneohe Bay, Hawaii in FY2023 increased MAGTF mobility and logistical capacity throughout the Indo-Pacific.

Praising the KC-130J's capabilities, Gering said: "The KC-130J has proven its value by operating from austere airfields in forward operating areas and providing mission support including emergency evacuation of personnel and key equipment, and special warfare operations.

As the sole USMC tactical fixed wing lift and aerial refuelling aircraft, demand for KC-130Js will remain high as a critical asset to the MAGTF and the Joint Force for the movement of aircraft and cargo.

VMGR squadrons are structured to support a home station element and one enduring three-aircraft detachment. The home station element is capable of dual shift maintenance, while the detachment is only single-shift maintenance-capable.

An additional deployable detachment to support simultaneous contingencies is a surge capability held by each VMGR, however, the squadron is not structured to sustain the additional detachment on an enduring basis.

Currently, marine aviation operates 75 KC-130J aircraft designated as the Primary Mission Aircraft Inventory (PMAI), ten are designated as Backup Aircraft

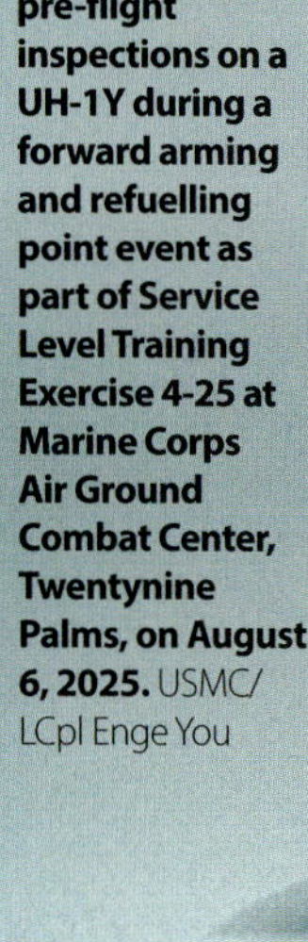

Below: **A crew chief conducts pre-flight inspections on a UH-1Y during a forward arming and refuelling point event as part of Service Level Training Exercise 4-25 at Marine Corps Air Ground Combat Center, Twentynine Palms, on August 6, 2025.** USMC/LCpl Enge You

Inventory (BAI), one is designated as Primary Development/Test Aircraft Inventory (PDAI), and nine are designated as attrition reserve yet to be funded. The US Marine Corps' KC-130J programme of record is 95 aircraft.

The KC-130J force comprises four active squadrons with 15 PMAI and two BAI; one reserve squadron with 15 PMAI and two BAI, and one test squadron with one PDAI.

Marine aviation's transition from the legacy KC-130R and KC-130T variants to the KC-130J began in 2000 and is scheduled to be complete in 2027.

Detailing upgrades for the KC-130J, Gering said: "Through co-ordination with the logistics and ground combat elements, we have begun redistributing capabilities like GPS retransmission kits and hatch-mounted satellite antenna system supply aircrew with real time data, which can be transferred in flight, providing MAGTF units the most accurate and up-to-date information. In addition, we have realigned aircrew training devices in accordance with Force Design and initial accession requirements, to support increased training demands following the stand-up of VMGR-153 and the possible expansion of KC-130J fleet replacement training."

Funding priorities for the KC-130J cited by Gering are common configuration

upgrades to hardware, software, processors, and terminals needed to integrate the MAGTF Agile Network Gateway Link, dubbed MANGL, and procurement of Large Aircraft Infrared Countermeasure (LAIRCM) kits.

MV-22B Osprey

Since the first deployment in 2007, the MV-22's revolutionary capability has been a cornerstone of the MAGTF, providing medium lift assault support to ground forces in multiple theatres of operation from expeditionary sites and afloat.

Gering said the MV-22 also provides unmatched operational flexibility due to its combination of speed, range, payload, and aerial refuelling capability. MV-22Bs currently based in Djibouti, Hawaii, and Okinawa, provide the ability to respond to crisis, contingencies, and humanitarian missions across large swaths of Africa, Asia, and the Indo-Pacific regions.

MV-22B squadrons have conducted a total of 109 operational deployments and flown over 588,000 flight hours since 2007. The MV-22 maintains mishap rates on par with other marine aviation aircraft and helicopters. As of August 1, 2024, the MV-22's ten-year (2014-2024) Class A mishap rate is 3.15 per every 100,000 flights hours, lower than the USMC average of 3.24 and lower than four other TMS aircraft.

Marine aviation has a programme of record for 360 MV-22Bs in the following squadron bed-down: 16 active squadrons with ten aircraft assigned; two reserve squadrons with ten aircraft each; one fleet replacement squadron (FRS) with assigned; one executive transport

detachment (det) with 12; one operational test det with five, and one developmental test det with four. Marine Medium Tiltrotor Squadron 264 (VMM-264) will reactivate in FY2026 and achieve initial operation capability in FY2027, the 16th squadron.

In less than two years, the MV-22B fleet halved the total number of unique configurations and reduced inventory from 12 to ten PAA per squadron. This yielded a versatile, relevant, deployable, and sustainable tiltrotor force postured for distributed aviation operations and in full support of Force Design.

Explaining the MV-22's relevance to marine aviation, Gering said: "As the core of the Marine Expeditionary Unit Aviation Combat Element and centrepiece of MAGTF amphibious lift, the Osprey must continue to evolve. Over the next two years we will focus on MV-22 capabilities, readiness, and sustainability for the growing fleet; modernisation improvements to improve reliability and capability to ensure platform relevance through fielding of next generation assault support; improving degraded visual environment [DVE] flight capabilities through development of a new flight control computer that improves aircraft handling qualities to alleviate aircrew workload in a DVE; aircraft survivability equipment upgrades; digital interoperability including the MAGTF Agile Network Gateway Link (MANGL) to bring on the Link-16 data link, and the ALQ-231 Intrepid Tiger II Block V electronic warfare system."

Following the November 29, 2023, crash of an Air Force Special Operations Command CV-22B Osprey at sea while on

Above: **A CH-53E Stallion assigned to Marine Heavy Helicopter Squadron 361 lands at Marine Corps Air-Ground Combat Center, Twentynine Palms, on July 28, 2025, during Service Level Training Exercise 4-25. SLTE is designed to be a challenging, realistic training environment that produces combat-ready forces capable of operating as an integrated MAGTF.** USMC/ LCpl Judith Ann Lazaro

Triple-melt steel is now the source material for the internal components of the PRGB which should drastically reduce the likelihood of material defects in critical gears and bearings.

CH-53E Super Stallion and CH-53K King Stallion

The CH-53K King Stallion offers three times the range and payload capacity of the CH-53E Super Stallion. It can transport heavy equipment, troops, and supplies over long distances, ensuring forces remain agile and supported. Operating from both land and sea bases, including austere sites and amphibious shipping, it provides crucial flexibility required by a MAGTF.

The brand-new CH-53K can carry both internal and external cargo loads and can

approach to Yakushima Airport, Japan, the USAF Accident Investigation Board identified a catastrophic failure of the left-hand proprotor gearbox (PRGB) which caused instant asymmetric lift, which made the aircraft roll twice before impacting the water. The CV-22B aircraft was destroyed and all eight crewmembers were killed. Consequently, the V-22 fleet was grounded until the entire US fleet was cleared to fly again with new restrictions issued in an interim flight clearance (IFC) on March 8, 2024. The USAF Accident Investigation Board issued its report on the accident near Yakushima, on August 1, 2024.

Flight safety concerns reemerged after an Air Force Special Operations Command CV-22B made a performed precautionary landing on November 20, 2024, during a local training mission from Cannon Air Force Base, New Mexico, which led to an operational pause for all V-22 variants. One month later, NAVAIR issued a fleet bulletin directing an inspection of V-22 Osprey aircraft to verify the flight hours on each PRGB prior to an aircraft's next flight.

As the largest operator of the V-22, the work being undertaken by marine aviation to integrate improvements to the PRGB, enhancing aircraft safety and improving component reliability and durability is considerable.

Osprey Drive System Safety and Health Instrumentation (ODSSHI – pronounced 'Odyssey'), includes sensors installed in critical areas of the PRGB and drive train. The sensors enable continuous drive system component monitoring for predictive maintenance actions prior to failure.

Above: **A UH-1Y assigned to Marine Light Attack Helicopter Squadron 369 takes off from the USS *Somerset* off the coast of California during Quarterly Underway Amphibious Readiness Training 25.4. This joint training exercise is designed to develop and sustain essential amphibious readiness skills for effective operations in maritime environments.** USMC/LCpl Alan Gomez

maintain performance in environments degraded by adverse weather, poor visibility, and contested areas. This versatility allows the massive helicopter to execute missions like combat assault transport, casualty evacuation, and logistical resupply.

A CH-53-equippped HMH squadron is designed to be task organised and is manned, trained and equipped with a Primary Mission Aircraft Authorization (PMAA) of 16 aircraft. An HMH can also operate as a temporary squadron with a Primary Mission Aircraft Inventory (PMAI) of 12 aircraft, or as an eight aircraft squadron with two simultaneous four aircraft detachments.

The current inventory of 127 aircraft is approximately 30 aircraft short of the required CH-53E fleet size. Prior to the arrival of the CH-53K, the shortage

Above: **A CH-53E Super Stallion assigned to Medium Tiltrotor Squadron 265 (Reinforced), 31st Marine Expeditionary Unit, takes off from the flight deck of USS America.** USN/MC SMN Sam McNeely

Left: **An F-35B assigned to Marine Fighter Attack Squadron 242, 31st Marine Expeditionary Unit, prepares to land on the flight deck of USS America, while conducting flight operations in the Philippine Sea.** USN/MC 3C Jeadan Andre

of CH-53E aircraft caused each HMH squadron to operate at threequarters the intended 16-aircraft PMAA. However, during FY2023 and FY2024 each CH-53E-equipped HMH squadron was returned to the full 16 PMAI strength, a revised posture enabled by fielding new CH-53Ks and the recapitalisation of CH-53E previously operated by the first transitioning squadron, HMH-461.

The USMC's CH-53K programme of record is 200 aircraft which will equip six active squadrons each with 16 CH-53Ks assigned, one reserve squadron also with 16, one fleet replacement squadron with 17 assigned, one operational test detachment equipped with two, and one developmental test detachment also with two CH-53Ks. The programme of record accounts for backup and attrition aircraft but is 20 aircraft short of the 220-requirement due to budget constraints.

Marine Heavy Helicopter Squadron 461 (HMH-461) completed its transition in approximately 24 months, and subsequent squadrons are expected to transition within 18-24 months each.

Gering said marine aviation had updated the initial CH-53K force structure laydown for stakeholders to ensure complete developmental and operational testing, as well as officer and enlisted student training. Marine Test and Evaluation Squadron 1 (VMX-1) and Helicopter Experimental Squadron 21 (HX-21) will have the necessary force structure to achieve the assigned tasks while building the inventory to staff Marine

Above: **An F-35B assigned to Marine Fighter Attack Squadron 242, 31st Marine Expeditionary Unit, takes-off from USS** *America* **in the Philippine Sea, on August 10, 2025.** USMC/LCpl Gerardo Mendez

priorities: digital interoperability, survivability and lethality, structural improvement, and an electrical power upgrade, dubbed STEPU, which provides greater electrical power capacity.

Investment in the AH-1Z and UH-1Y over the next two FYDPs is essential to maintaining a ready crisis response force, pivotal to reduce risk in the development of the H-1 Next, and critical to bridge the gap for the MAGTF as it transforms into a fully modernised fleet.

Marine aviation funding priorities for the H-1 include digital interoperability, to improve survivability with the integration of the Distributed Aperture Infrared Countermeasure (DAIRCM) with dual lasers and the APR-39D(V)2 digital radar warning receiver, the SIEPU, and integration of position, navigation, and timing (PNT) technologies for all weather navigation.

Gering's plan also included details of marine aviation's support aircraft used for adversary and operational support.

F-5 Tiger II

Marine aviation operates two variants of the Northrop F-5 Tiger – the single-seat F-5N, former Swiss Air Force aircraft, and the two-seat F-5F for fixed-wing aggressor training for TACAIR, assault support, ground-based air defence (GBAD), and Marine Air Control Squadron requirements. The F-5 mission objective is to enhance the combat readiness of marine aviation and other elements of the MAGTF.

Thirteen F-5s are assigned to Marine Fighter Training Squadron 401 (VMFT-401) based at Yuma, Arizona and VMFT-402 at Beaufort, South Carolina. Currently, the F-5 programme of record is 22 F-5s with delivery spread over the next four years.

The F-5 fleet is funded for life-limited components such as upper cockpit longerons, wings, horizontal stabilator pairs, and vertical stabilators that will enable the F-5F aircraft to achieve the planned 6,000-hour service life and 9,000 hours for the F-5N.

Marine aviation F-5s are currently undergoing a glass cockpit upgrade at a rate of two to three aircraft per year. Red Net, a tactical data link upgrade which enhances the ability to simulate threats in training scenarios, and the integration of the Tactical Combat Training System Increment II, an air combat training system which enhances training realism and interoperability, will allow synthetic adversary to be input to the training scenario to reduce the forecasted gap in adversary training.

According to Gering, the use of commercial contractors to provide adversary support cannot satisfy all marine aviation's adversary requirements. With the stand-up of VMFT-402 at Beaufort, the additional live capacity in the F-5 fleet will complement marine aviation's exploration of low-cost training opportunities, incorporating live, virtual, constructive capabilities, and commercial air services to augment requirements.

Operational Support Airlift

Marine aviation's airlift, known as operational support airlift (OSA) provides its forces and MAGTFs with time-sensitive air transport of high priority passengers, cargo, and other critical air logistic support.

OSA is a critical enabler for the success of forward deployed MAGTFs and has been continuously deployed since 2004. Today, OSA aircraft are currently supporting Marine Corps Forces Central

Below: **Marines prepare to attach simulated cargo to a CH-53E Super Stallion helicopter assigned to Marine Heavy Helicopter Squadron 462 during an external lift exercise at a landing zone on Okinawa, Japan.** USMC/LCpl Eric Reyes

As marine aviation continues its transition to the F-35, their requirement for sorties involving adversary support will increase to nearly 1,800 sorties per year. The two F-35B training squadrons are Marine Fighter Attack Training Squadron 501 (VMFAT-501) based at Beaufort, and VMFAT-502 based at Miramar. The annual requirement for sorties requiring adversary support is expected to increase for transitioning F-35 squadrons from 12,000 in FY2022 to 17,000 to meet fleet training requirements.

Above: **A plane captain salutes the pilot of an F-35C assigned to Marine Fighter Attack Squadron 251 before a mission during Exercise Red Flag-Nellis 25-3 at Nellis Air Force Base on July 22, 2025.** USAF/ William Lewis

Command and Marine Forces Europe and Africa Command.

The active component provides OSA support from each Marine Corps Air Station, while the OSA reserves unit, Marine Transport Squadron 1 (VMR-1) assigned to the 4th Marine Air Wing, based at Belle Chasse, Louisiana, and Andrews, Maryland, is critical to support time-sensitive logistics requirements.

In addition to augmenting and reinforcing the active component OSA communities, the 4th MAW is established as the TMS lead for three of the four OSA aircraft, the UC-12W, UC-35D, and C-40A.

VMR-1 now operates a C-40A to provide rapid inter-theatre transportation to marines and supports the 'fight tonight' mindset championed by Force Design.

Marine aviation's top OSA priority is to recapitalise all non-deployable UC-12F, UC-12M and UC-35D aircraft with investment in the UC-12W, 12 of which are currently in service of a total of 30 aircraft.

Gering's plan also included details of marine aviation's presidential helicopter fleet.

VH-3D and VH-60N

Marine Helicopter Squadron 1 (HMX-1) based at Quantico, Virginia, has a specific mission set that includes transportation for the President of the United States around the world and transportation within the National Capital Region for the Vice President, members of the President's cabinet, and visiting heads of state. In addition, HMX-1 continues to conduct operational test and evaluation for rotary wing Presidential lift aircraft.

The squadron is currently transitioning from legacy VH-3D and VH-60N aircraft to the VH-92A. The US Marine Corps declared initial operational capability for the VH-92A in December 2021 and HMX-1 began its introduction into operational missions in 2022 following White House commissioning events.

VH-3D and VH-60N helicopters have undergone a service life extension programme and have sufficient hours to support the mission through the full transition to the VH-92A. The VH-3D and VH-60N helicopters will be retired as they reach airframe hour limits and as the VH-92A takes on more of the mission. VH-3D aircraft are anticipated to continue serving through 2026. Due to

Left: **Pilots assigned to HMX-1 run a test flight of the new VH-92A over the south lawn of the White House on September 22, 2018, Washington DC.** USMC/Sgt Hunter Helis

Below: **An F-35C assigned to Marine Fighter Attack Squadron 251 based at Marine Corps Air Station Cherry Point taxis out for a mission in support of Red Flag-Nellis 25-3 at Nellis Air Force Base on July 22, 2025.** USAF/William Lewis

the VH-3D's unique capabilities in high/hot environments, the VH-60N aircraft are anticipated to continue serving through 2030 before being fully retired.

There are no major upgrades currently planned for either aircraft. However, minor communications upgrades may be necessary to ensure the remaining legacy aircraft are operationally relevant until the squadron has completely transitioned to the VH-92A.

VH-92A

The White House Military Office Transition Plan stipulates an event-driven, multi-phased approach to replace legacy aircraft with the VH-92A, of which there currently ten assigned to support mission tasking.

Marine aviation's VH-92A programme of record is for 23 aircraft, all of which have been produced: the final aircraft was accepted in August 2024. Once HMX-1 has fully transitioned and divested its legacy

Above: **An F-35C assigned to Marine Fighter Attack Squadron 314 launches off the flight deck of the USS *Abraham Lincoln*.** USN/MC SMN Shepard Fosdyke-Jackson

VH-3D and VH-60N helicopters, it will operate 16 VH-92As.

Despite the early stage of its service career, marine aviation is already investing in the VH-92A to improve aircraft performance in hot and high environments and to increase available bandwidth in the aircraft using beyond-line-of-sight systems.

Aviation Weapons

Marine aviation weapon development is focused on increasing lethality and survivability by leveraging increased range, speed, and digital interoperability. Trying to build an effective weapons inventory when faced with budget restrictions requires a balance between procuring new advanced weapons designed to target and attrite an adversary's most capable threats and having enough weapons suitable for prolonged conflicts. Striking a balance tends to direct procurement strategies and priorities for both air-to-ground and air-to-air weapons.

Long Range Anti-Ship Missile (LRASM)

The AGM-158C LRASM is a long-range, precision-guided, anti-ship cruise missile designed to engage ships in a highly contested environment. LRASM utilises semi-autonomous engagement to increase the stand-off range for the aircraft launch platform, to improve survivability and lethality above that of legacy maritime strike weapons.

The LRASM C-1 variant was operationally fielded on USN F/A-18E and F/A-18F Super Hornets in FY2024, but the integration effort for the F-35B and F-35C continues. The C-1 variant is projected to achieve international operational capacity (IOC) on the F-35B and F-35C for external carriage in early FY2026. Concurrent to aircraft integration, the LRASM C-3 variant is in development to field on the F-35 fleet in FY2028. Once fielded, the LRASM will enhance the power projection and sea control provided by aircraft operating from expeditionary air bases and CVN- and L-class carriers.

Stand-off and Net-Enabled Weapons

Development and integration of the AGM-88E Advanced Anti-Radiation Guided Missile-Extended Range (AARGM-ER) on the F-35 fleet is a priority. The F-35 JPO simultaneously worked on integrating the AARGM-ER on the F-35 aircraft with the intent to accelerate fielding using internal carriage on the F-35C, followed by integration on the F-35B using external carriage.

SHOOTER
300

Integration of the GBU-53/B Small Diameter Bomb II on the F-35B and F-35C continues, with IOC projected in early FY2025 with the release of OFP 30P08.

Internal carriage of up to eight GBU-53/B weapons will significantly increase target per sortie ratios and enable greater flexible weapon-to-target pairings than traditional laser-guided and Joint Direct Attack Munitions (JDAM) series bombs.

The GBU-53/B is expected to be the first net-enabled weapon fielded on the F-35B and F-35C variants. GBU-53/B is a joint programme with the USAF and is expected to advance guidance and communication capabilities via incremented configuration changes to ensure the weapon maintains lethality against pacing threats.

AGM-179 Joint Air-to-Ground Missile

In March 2022, the AGM-179 Joint Air-to-Ground Missile (JAGM) achieved IOC on the AH-1Z and became the first true fire-and-forget air-to-ground capability for the H-1 fleet. The missile enhances an AH-1Z's flexibility and lethality in contested environments, and will receive incremental upgrades, including funded efforts to add counter-UAS software and the integration of a new electromagnetic control actuator section. The counter-UAS software upgrade improves air-to-air guidance, and the laser pulse logic will increase engagement capability against a wide variety of adversary unmanned systems.

AGR-20 Advanced Precision Kill Weapon System II

Marine aviation's AGR-20 Advanced Precision Kill Weapon System II (APKWS II) provides a reliable, high-capacity precision-guided munition for both rotary wing and fixed wing types.

The APKWS programme has completely transitioned to the single variant block upgrade that enables the same guidance unit to be used for any platform, as well as increases the overall employment envelope. To improve performance against unmanned aerial systems, certification of a suitable proximity fuse is in development for fielding to the fleet with current guidance and warhead combinations.

Other demonstrations with the US Army and USAF are used to determine the feasibility of adding additional guidance methods to the APKWS family, including passive infrared seekers.

Above: **Sailors conduct final checks on an F-35C assigned to Marine Fighter Attack Squadron 314 prior to launch from the flight deck of the USS *Abraham Lincoln*.** USN/MC SMN Shepard Fosdyke-Jackson

Left: **A powerline mechanic assigned to Marine Fighter Attack Squadron 251 inspects an F-35C prior to a mission during Exercise Red Flag-Nellis 25-3 at Nellis Air Force Base, on July 22, 2025. The exercise provided the squadron the opportunity to co-ordinate with USAF KC-135 Stratotanker and KC-46 Pegasus tankers to refine aerial refuelling procedures critical to enable long-range F-35C operations.** USAF/A1C Jennifer Nesbitt

Above: **An F-35C pilot and a powerline mechanic, both assigned to Marine Fighter Attack Squadron 251 prepare an F-35C before a mission at Nellis Air Force Base, on July 22, 2025. Red Flag builds joint combat readiness by integrating marine pilots into realistic, high-threat scenarios, testing their expeditionary reach and rapid deployment capability.** USAF/A1C Jennifer Nesbitt

Precision Attack Strike Missile

The Precision Attack Strike Missile (PASM) is a long-range, surface-to-surface missile developed by the US Army to replace the ageing Army Tactical Missile System dubbed ATACMS.

Marine aviation is conducting a joint capability technology demonstration for a long-range attack weapon, formally known as the Long-Range Attack Missile.

PASM has successfully been launched from the AH-1Z, with continued testing undertaken to prove the technological capability and operational value of helicopters armed with advanced weapons for offensive anti-surface warfare or maritime strike.

The AIM-9X Block II Sidewinder and AIM-120 AMRAAM air-to-air missile programs continue to modernise each weapon. A system improvement programme (SIP) for the AIM- 9X includes both software and hardware upgrades, including a new digital fuse to replace the current DSU-41 active optical target detector. A similar SIP for the AIM-120D-3 variant includes significant hardware upgrades as part of the overarching form, fit, and function refresh initiative.

Annual weapons training allocations and expenditures are a priority. Marine aviation must balance the current year's training requirements with the need to maintain sufficient weapon inventories for contingencies. Changes have been made to how the non-combat weapons expenditure allocation is developed each year to manage the available inventory and maximise training opportunities year after year. Various requirements – training and readiness, weapons schools, service level training exercises, and military occupational specialty school support – account for a significant portion of the ordnance requirements to sustain fleet readiness and proficiency.

Digital Interoperability

Getting the required information to the right participants at the right time to overcome an adversary is the objective for achieving digital interoperability (DI) in a MAGTF. As the principle USMC organisation structured to conduct a wide range of operations, MAGTFs operate in ever increasing distributed and disaggregated environments in which efficient flow of data and information is critical.

Marine aviation meets this requirement by using a digital link dubbed DI MANGL or MAGTF Agile Network Gateway Link. It's a proven system that connects multiple disparate or stove-piped sensor and communications systems using integrated networks. This feeds situational awareness to units across the MAGTF, naval, joint, and collation domains via a common interface. The system adds speed and range to a MAGTF's combined arms capability without requiring a man-in-the-loop to manage the data and detract from the existing mission essential tasks.

The lead type for DI MANGL is the MV-22B Osprey, with a demonstration planned to take place in late FY2026, followed by a fielding decision in FY2027. Integration efforts of DI MANGL to the KC-130J and CH-53K are also underway.

Aircraft Survivability Equipment

Advanced anti-aircraft threats and integrated air defences, including dual-mode detection, and tracking across the electromagnetic spectrum requires robust aircraft survivability equipment (ASE) on all aircraft, helicopters, and tiltrotors that can detect, identify, and defeat such systems. Current systems used by marine aviation aircraft, helicopters, and tiltrotors are:

The AAR-47 missile warning system (MWS) which detects infrared guided missiles, laser-guided weapons, and unguided munitions. This system provides audio and visual warnings to aircrews and automatically dispenses expendable countermeasures. The AAR-47 is integrated on KC-130J, AH-1Z, UH-1Y, CH-53E, and MV-22B aircraft, and is being replaced by more advanced systems.

Right: **Colonel William Mitchell, the commanding officer of Marine Aircraft Group 11, conducts final inspections on an F/A-18C Hornet assigned to Marine Fighter Attack Squadron 323 before his final flight at Marine Corps Air Station Miramar, on June 25, 2025.** USMC/LCpl Samantha Devine

Above: **A test engineer assigned to Marine Operational Test and Evaluation Squadron 1 signals to the pilot of an F-35B during an Expeditionary Advanced Base Operations risk reduction effort at Marine Corps Air Station Yuma. The purpose of the risk reduction effort was to inform flight clearance operations for short landings and take-offs on prepared and semi-prepared surfaces in support of the squadron's EABO exercise Operation Obsidian Iceberg.** USMC/LCpl Jade Venegas

The AAQ-24 Large Aircraft Infrared Countermeasure (LAIRCM) is an advanced MWS with laser warning and hostile fire indicator capabilities. This system provides situational awareness, inexhaustible, directed-energy laser countermeasures to defeat infrared-guided missiles, and automatically dispenses expendable countermeasures. The AAQ-24 is replacing the AAR-47 on KC-130J, CH-53E, and MV-22 aircraft, and is integrated on the CH-53K.

The AAQ-45 Distributed Aperture Infrared Countermeasure (DAIRCM) is a lightweight MWS that provides situational awareness, automatically dispenses expendable countermeasures, and inexhaustible directed-energy laser countermeasures. The latest version features improved sensors with additional digital interoperability. The AAQ-45 replaces the AAR-47 on AH-1Z and UH-1Y aircraft.

The APR-39 radar warning receiver (RWR) provides radar threat detection and integrates with other systems. The updated APR-39D(V)2 features an interface with the ALE-47 countermeasure dispensing set (CMDS), digital receivers, improved probability of detection of threats, increased reporting accuracy and improved displays. The system is integrated on KC-130J, AH-1Z, AH-1Y, CH-53E, CH-53K and MV-22B aircraft.

The ALE-47 CMDS is an integrated, threat-adaptive, reprogrammable system for dispensing expendable decoys, one that receives threat data and navigational inputs to optimise countermeasure response. The ALE-47 is integrated on KC-130J, AH-1Z, AH-1Y, CH-53E, CH-53K, F/A-18C, F/A-18D, and MV-22B aircraft.

The ALR-67 RWR detects, identifies, and displays radars and radar-guided weapon systems. It provides radar threat information to the ALE-47 for optimised countermeasures dispensation, and operates in co-ordination with onboard fire control radars, datalinks, jammers, missile detection systems, and anti-radiation missiles. The ALR-67 system is integrated on F/A-18C and F/A-18D aircraft.

The ALQ-214 Integrated Defense Electronic Countermeasure IDECM provides self-protection against surface-to-air and air-to-air missiles. The V5 is an improved version designed to enhance interoperability and multi-threat engagement. The ALQ-214 is integrated on F/A-18C and F/A-18D aircraft.

In the future, marine aviation will field a common carriage system to increase the number of expendable countermeasures carried by the CH-53K and MV-22B aircraft. The system uses square expendables that are common with those used by the F-35 and compatible with advanced RF (radio frequency) and EO-IR (electro-optical/infrared) expendables under development. Further funding for the next generation pointer/tracker is expected to improve current and future infrared countermeasure systems. A pointer/tracker directs the laser countermeasures at a threat missile's infrared seeker to dazzle its guidance ability.

Enabling Marine Aviation

For all the aircraft, helicopters and tiltrotors in the world, their individual and collective mission effectiveness would be next to zero without the organisations that enable them to take-off on the next mission.

In the expeditionary context, Marine Air Control Groups (MACG) and Marine Wing Support Squadrons (MWSS) are the primary expeditionary enablers. The MACG and MWSS provide an aviation command and control and ground support (AC2GS) system which is unique in the joint force, optimises the control of aircraft and missiles, and facilitates aviation operations from austere sites.

Marine aviation enablers also reside in Littoral Anti-Air Battalions (LAAB), units designed to provide air defence, surveillance, and early warning capabilities in coastal (littoral) regions. A LAAB provides multi-domain command and control and integrates multi-domain fires.

Highlighting the contributions made by expeditionary enablers, Gering said: "The ability to control and defend our own airspace, execute combat identification, close kill chains and enable kill webs, provide all weather air traffic control [ATC] and precision recovery services, provide ground-based air defence, and provide aviation ground support activities continue to be in high demand."

Aviation ground support (AGS) comprises the tailored engineering and logistics capabilities required to sustain air operations at expeditionary land bases, but excludes supply, maintenance, and ordnance. AGS is provided by an MWSS which has capability to conduct landing zone survey and construction, contingency airfield support, airfield assessment and repair, aircraft salvage and recovery, and forward arming and refuelling point operations to directly support all functions of marine aviation.

Three of the most fascinating systems used by an MWSS in the provision of AGS are explained below.

Marine aviation is procuring 52 Vertical Take Off and Landing (VTOL) surfacing systems to support Expeditionary Air Base Operations. Procurement with full operating capability is expected in FY2029.

The branch is modernising its expeditionary airfield lighting capability with LED-equipped CAT I lights, which support precision instrument approaches and include improvements for STOVL (short take-off vertical landings) and VTOL landings. Test systems have been installed at Marine Corps Auxiliary Landing Field Bogue, North Carolina, the Strategic Expeditionary Landing Field at Twentynine Palms, California, and the Marine Corps Mountain Warfare Training Center Bridgeport, California. Each of the three Marine Air Wings will be equipped with one system with an expected full operational capability (FOC) in FY2026.

Forward Arming and Refuelling Point operations are supported by an air-transportable ULTV (Ultra-Light Tactical Vehicle) trailer-mounted Tactical Aviation and Ground Refuelling System which has two points for simultaneous refuelling. IOC was achieved in FY2024, and FOC is projected for FY2026.

Aviation Training Systems

Like any air force, training is critical to marine aviation, not least because the service operates a diverse range of types: unmanned aerial vehicles to fast

Right: Marines with Marine Wing Support Squadron 471 install AM-2 matting panels during repair operations to the Strategic Expeditionary Landing Field at Marine Air Ground Combat Center Twentynine Palms. AM-2 matting panels are reusable steel epoxy-coated panels that are connected to create expeditionary airfields. USMC/Sgt Booker Thomas

Below: Marines assigned to Marine Wing Support Squadron 471 transport AM-2 matting at the Strategic Expeditionary Landing Field at Marine Air-Ground Combat Center Twentynine Palms. The matting offers exceptional versatility and rapid installation, which significantly minimises the transition time from construction to aviation operations. USMC/ Sgt Booker Thomas

jets. To support the constant training requirement, an aviation training system integrates training processes and structures into a single, unified, and holistic system that spans all aircraft – helicopter, tiltrotor, and unmanned types.

The system also integrates and co-ordinates policy, manpower, equipment, facilities, and fiscal requirements for officers and enlisted personnel. Plus, it integrates aircrew training for squadrons that conduct platform-specific aviation training, for example, the MV-22 fleet replacement squadron, Marine Medium Tiltrotor Training Squadron 204 (VMMT-204) based at New River, North Carolina.

Concepts, processes, and programs used by the system are applicable to all current and future marine aviation training programs, including naval and/ or joint programs in which marine aviation participates. Implementation and operational control of air traffic service (ATS) resides with each Marine Air Wing: 1st MAW based at Futenma, Okinawa; 2nd MAW based at Cherry Point, North Carolina; 3rd based at Miramar, California; and the 4th MAW based at Belle Chase, Louisiana.

Simulators

Simulators are specifically designed to train aircrew, maintainers, and marines who work in command and control in the execution of training and readiness events.

Aircrew simulators are categorised as:
Aircrew procedures trainer
Flight training device
Containerised flight training device

Weapons systems trainer
Tactical operational flight trainer
Full flight simulator
Full mission simulator
Aircrew training aid
Deployable mission rehearsal trainer
Mission rehearsal trainer
Cockpit procedures trainer

Enlisted aircrew/crew simulators are categorised as:
Fuselage trainer
Observer training aid
Marine common aircrew trainer

Maintenance simulators represent various aircraft systems and components particular to each type-model-series aircraft.

By 2030, marine aviation plans to add an additional 24 aircrew simulators, two enlisted aircrew/crew simulators, and ten maintenance simulators/training devices.

Noteworthy is the incorporation of deployable trainers, shifting the training focus to battle management, combat situational awareness, and co-ordinated fires rather than on basic flight skills.

Marine aviation also uses live, virtual, and constructive (LVC) training which is a blended training approach that combines real-world activities (live), simulated environments (virtual), and computer-generated forces (constructive) to create a more comprehensive and effective training experience. The use of LVC enhances fleet training with the ability of simulating and integrating advanced systems into realistic threat environments.

The Aviation Distributed Virtual Training Environment (ADVTE) is a system used by marine aviation that links geographically dispersed flight simulators to enable realistic training and mission rehearsals. ADVTE uses local and wide area networks to connect simulators across different locations.

ADVTE integrates all marine aviation aircraft, helicopters, tiltrotors and systems into a common training environment, and work is underway to connect MAGTF ground training devices with the ADVTE to conduct training events and exercises as a MAGTF. ADVTE is also interoperable with similar virtual training environments operated by the USAF and USN.

Marine Aviation Ranges

As America's expeditionary force at readiness, the USMC and marine aviation hold combined-arms capabilities and specialise in amphibious operation. Various weapons and munitions are employed by the service which, in the case of marine aviation, requires ranges to practise live and inert weapons employment. There are two primary USMC ranges: the Townsend bombing range, Georgia, and the Yuma training area, Arizona. Two joint electronic warfare ranges are also used: the Mid Atlantic Electronic Warfare Range (MAEWR), North Carolina, and the Southwest Tactical Training Range (SWTTR), Arizona.

Encompassing almost 34,000 acres located in coastal Georgia, approximately 82 miles from Beaufort, the Townsend

Below: **An F-5N Tiger II assigned to Marine Fighter Training Squadron 402 (VMFT-402) at its home station, Marine Corps Air Station Beaufort, South Carolina, on May 22, 2025.** USMC/LCpl Kayla LeClaire

Right: A marine assigned to Marine Wing Support Squadron 371 tows a tactical aviation ground refuelling system to a forward arming and refuelling point event during a Weapons and Tactics Instructor course. USMC/LCpl Shannon Gibson

bombing range (TBR) is the primary training range for the F-35, 2nd MAW, and various US Army, US Navy, and US Air Force units. Marine squadrons use the TBR to fire cannons using inert rounds, rockets, general purpose bombs, and precision munitions such as JADMs and laser-guided bombs. The TBR can also accommodate limited advanced weapon deliveries normally requiring deployment to ranges in Arizona and California.

The USMC premier range is the Yuma training range (YTA) which encompasses several million acres of southwestern desert. The vast size of the YTA's airspace and underlying range impact and manoeuvre areas, permits use of the latest weapons and tactics. This gives marine aviators the ability to conduct training in the way they will fight. MCAS Yuma supports 80% of marine aviation's air-to-ground training.

Electronic warfare (EW) training is gained at either the MAEWR and the SWTTR, each range is equipped with the necessary systems and equipment required for EW training. Threat systems and capabilities are replicated across the RF spectrum

to acquire, track, target, and engage aircraft. Modern EW systems require the greatest level of fidelity to replicate threat signals and processes to allow aviators to experience the challenge of being engaged by a realistic integrated threat system.

Above: **Marines assigned to the 31st Marine Expeditionary Unit prepare to load an AIM-9X missile on the flight deck of the USS *America* while in the Philippine Sea on June 3, 2025.** USN/MC 2C Cole Pursley

Left: **Aviation ordnance system technicians assigned to Marine Aviation Logistics Squadron 12 move an inert GBU-31 Joint Direct Attack Munition in support of Marine Air Group 12's Aviation Training Relocation Program at Tinian, Northern Mariana Islands, on January 27, 2025.** USMC/LCpl Dahkareo Pritchett

Marine aviation procures training aircraft with the USN to support undergraduate flight training managed by the Chief of Naval Aviation Training (CNATRA). Four types of trainer aircraft (T-6A Texan II, T-44A Pegasus, T-45 Goshawk, T-54A Marlin II, and TH-73A Thrasher), associated simulators, academic publications, computer-based training systems, assigned to six wings are used to train USN and USMC aircrew.

The T-6A Texan II is one component of the Joint Primary Aircraft Training System (JPATS) along with simulators, computer-aided academics.

The T-44A Pegasus is used for advanced turboprop aircraft training and for intermediate E-2 Hawkeye (carrier-based turboprop radar aircraft) training. This aircraft is equipped with de-icing and anti-icing systems augmented by instrumentation and navigation equipment to allow for flight under instrument and icing conditions. The T-44A Pegasus is being replaced by the Beechcraft King Air 360-based T-54A Marlin II.

The T-45 Goshawk is used for intermediate and advanced portions of the CNATRA aircrew training programme for jet carrier aviation and tactical missions.

The TH-73A Thrasher (based on the AgustaWestland AW119) is the aircraft portion of the Advanced Helicopter Training System (AHTS) for helicopter and tiltrotor pilots. The cab is equipped with a modern digital cockpit, and the AHTS uses for a modern training curriculum that reflects the capabilities of marine aviation's current inventory.

Marine Aviation Reserve

One of marine aviation's Marine Aircraft Wings, the 4th based at Belle Chase, Louisiana, is a reserve organisation, but one that remains ready, relevant, and responsive to any threat.

Outlining the wing, Gering said: "The 4th MAW functions as an operational MAW integrating three core capabilities: aircraft operations, aviation ground support and aviation command and control. Within all its groups, 4th MAW deploys units, detachments, and individual augments across the range of military operations in support of contingency operations, the Unit Deployment Program (UDP), Combatant Commanders' Theater Security Co-operation (TSC) missions, joint and service level operations, and training exercises."

Marines assigned to the Marine Aviation Logistics Squadrons (MALS) within the 4th MAW work with 1st, 2nd, and 3rd MAW units to leverage and incorporate the capability of the total force. Each MALS provides aviation logistics support, planning and guidance to aviation squadrons assigned to a Marine Aircraft Group on behalf of the commanding officer.

During Exercise RIMPAC 2024, 4th MAW deployed marines from MALS-41 and MALS-49 to Marine Corps Base Hawaii to augment the resident MALS-24. At a time of high operational tempo, the 4th MAW marines reduced the overall stress on the unit to meet demand.

Following the relocation of MALS-49 from Newburgh, New York to New River, North Carolina, 4th MAW will strengthen ties with the active component by integrating with MALS-26 and providing unparalleled support.

The 4th MAW's only fighter squadron, VMFA-112 based at Joint Reserve Base Fort Worth, Texas, continues to support F/A-18 aircrews transferring from the active squadrons to the reserve component. VMFA-112 also provides augmentation and relief to support marine aviation commitments and the TACAIR transition plan. The 4th MAW will provide F/A-18s as a reserve capability until VMFA-112 transitions to the F-35C Lightning II in FY2031 and FY2032.

VMGR-234 based at Joint Reserve Base Fort Worth, started its transition from KC-130Ts to KC-130Js in March 2014 and will reach FOC upon delivery of its 15th aircraft planned for FY2027. The squadron regularly supports the reserve and active force with assault support requests and deployment augmentation.

Both reserve MV-22B-equipped VMM squadrons, VMM-764 and VMM-774, are co-located with active component MAGs which streamlines the logistics supply chain and increases interoperability with other tenant fleet squadrons assigned to the MAGs. VMM-764 is based at Miramar and VMM-774 is based at New River.

In FY2024, HMH-772, based at Joint Base McGuire, New Jersey, completed acceptance of its eighth CH-53E aircraft bringing the squadron to full strength and is poised to provide support around the world. Assessment is underway to determine if HMH-772 will increase from 8 to 16 CH-53E aircraft as early as FY2028, followed by transition to 16 CH-53Ks in FY2032. Infrastructure, basing, and personnel requirements for both transitions are under analysis.

The 4th MAW's MACG-48, MWSS-471, MWSS-472 and MWSS-473 have not undergone the same organisation changes as the active component. The MWSS squadrons retained all 571 personnel and MACG-48 retains the only Marine Tactical Air Command Squadron in the marine corps. All four units continue to serve as a highly effective backstop for the active

Above: **Marine One flies over Pike Field during the Army 250 celebration at Fort Bragg, North Carolina on June 10, 2025, with President Donald Trump on board.** US Army/SSgt Cory Reese

Below: **A crew chief working for a contractor inspects a UC-12W at Marine Corps Air Station Iwakuni, Japan, prior to departure.** USMC/ Cpl Mitchell Austin

Above: **President Barack Obama and Michelle Obama, the first lady, step off a VH-3D at Joint Base Andrews, Maryland, greeted by Colonel John Millard, then 89th Airlift Wing commander, and his wife, on September 23, 2014.** USAF/MSgt Kevin Wallace

component and often augment the active force during exercises and operations.

An MACG is responsible for providing, operating, and maintaining the Marine Air Command and Control System (MACCS) to ensure effective co-ordination and communication for air operations.

An MWSS is an aviation ground support unit that provides essential logistical and engineering support to Marine Aircraft Wings, ensuring the smooth operation of airfields and aircraft. An MWSS undertakes airfield construction and repair, fuel and power support, and various logistical tasks.

Marine Aviation Weapons and Tactics Squadron 1

Based at Yuma, Arizona, Marine Aviation Weapons and Tactics Squadron 1

(MAWTS-1) provides standardised advanced tactical training and certification of unit instructor qualifications through its Weapons and Tactics Instructor course (WTI). The squadron is marine aviation's weapon school and helps develop and employ aviation weapons and tactics in co-ordination with Marine Operational Test and Evaluation Squadron One (VMX-1).

The WTI course equips aviators, aviation planners, and critical enablers with superior tactical preparation skills and provides the Fleet Marine Force the most realistic, advanced, tactical training deemed as being required to succeed in both competition and conflict. MAWTS-1 relentlessly pursues excellence in all its students with a focus on preparedness.

MAWTS-1 focuses on advanced tactics that are informed by knowledge of the current and future threat. The squadron continually refines tactical problem sets in both size and scope. Currently, distributed joint operations are a focal point as students and instructors include maritime strike, tactical recovery of aircraft and personnel and close air support, both in a contested environment.

Right: **An MV-22B Osprey assigned to Medium Tiltrotor Squadron 265 (Reinforced), 31st Marine Expeditionary Unit on the flight deck of the forward-deployed amphibious assault ship USS** *America,* **while conducting flight operations in the Philippine Sea, on August 10, 2025.** USN/MC SMN Nicholas Douglass

Marine Operational Test and Evaluation Squadron 1

Also based at Yuma, Marine Operational Test and Evaluation Squadron 1 (VMX-1) conducts operational test and evaluation of all marine aviation platforms under the authority of Director, Operational Test and Evaluation Force (OPTEVFOR) or Director, Marine Corps Operational Test and Evaluation Activity (MCOTEA). VMX-1 creates, documents, and disseminates initial tactics, techniques and procedures for marine aviation platforms and systems. In coordination with MAWTS-1, VMX-1 supports concept development and refinement of tactics, techniques, and procedures. Additionally, the squadron co-ordinates and conducts government-sponsored experimentation and tactical demonstrations as directed by the Deputy Commandant Aviation.

Outlining the squadron's organisation, Gering said: "VMX-1 is staffed with experienced aircrew and maintainers to support the operational test of key marine capabilities. In June 2024, the CH-53K detachment then at New River re-joined the squadron at Yuma. Equipped with uniquely instrumented aircraft and an organic C4I department, VMX-1 conducts operational test to ensure emergent capabilities are appropriately vetted for both effectiveness and suitability in realistic combat environments.

"In addition, VMX-1 collaborates with MAWTS-1 and numerous Department of Defense innovation centres to ensure marine aviation is at the forefront of warfighting modernisation. These partnerships enable VMX-1 to rapidly iterate and inform EABO and DAO concepts. VMX-1 also integrates across the joint and partner force to increase interoperability and expedite the development of new technologies and tactics for the Fleet Marine Forces."

In 2025, VMX-1 is conducting operational test and evaluation on systems and weapons for the F-35B, AH-1Z, UH-1Y, CH-53K, MV-22B and the MQ-9A, all from Yuma. The squadron is also conducting multiple detachments and limited deployments to evaluate new technologies and will continue to partner with sister-service operational test organisations, tri-service weapons schools, and government research organisations. In May, VMX-1 participated in a major joint exercise at Nellis Air Force Base, Nevada that involved test squadrons from all US armed services.

Above: **An aviation boatswain's mate assigned to the forward-deployed amphibious assault ship USS *America*, signals to the pilot of an F-35B for take-off during flight operations in the Philippine Sea, on August 10, 2025.** USN/MC 2C Cole Pursley

CARRIER
AIR WING
TIP OF THE SPEAR

A review of the US Navy's nine Carrier Air Wings, notable aspects of their deployments in 2024-20[...]
and an overview of their deployment work-up training process.

NINE CARRIER AIR Wings (CVWs) are currently established in the US Navy (USN). Four are assigned to Commander, Naval Air Forces Atlantic (COMAIRLANT) and all are based at Naval Air Station Oceana, Virginia. On America's west coast, four more carrier air wings are assigned to Commander, Naval Air Force Pacific all based at Naval Air Station Lemoore, California.

The ninth CVW is also assigned to COMAIRPAC but is forward deployed to Marine Corps Air Station Iwakuni, Japan.

A CVW typically comprises nine flying squadrons: four strike fighter squadrons (VFA), one electronic attack squadron (VAQ), one airborne command and control squadron (VAW), one helicopter sea combat squadron (HSC), and a helicopter maritime strike squadron (HSM). Additionally, a detachment from a fleet logistics support squadron (VRC) or a fleet logistics multi-mission squadron (VRM).

Strike fighter squadrons operate either F/A-18 Super Hornets or F-35C Lightnings, all electronic attack squadrons fly EA-18G Growlers, airborne command and control squadrons operate E-2 Hawkeyes, helicopter sea combat squadrons fly MH-60S Seahawks, dubbed Sierras, and helicopter maritime strike squadrons operate MH-60R Seahawks dubbed Romeos.

Each CVW is assigned to a nuclear-powered aircraft carrier (CVN) either a Nimitz- or Ford-class ship. Nimitz is reference to the first-in-class USS *Nimitz*, CVN 68, and Ford is reference to the first-in-class USS *Gerald R Ford*, CVN 78.

The following overviews provide an insight to the latest deployments by each of the nine CVWs embarked on their assigned carrier.

The first five CVWs listed are those assigned to Commander, Naval Air Forces

Above: **Landing Signal Officers aboard the world's largest aircraft carrier, USS *Gerald R. Ford*, guide an F/A-18F Super Hornet in for a landing.** USN/ MC Seaman Apprentice Alyssa Joy

Pacific (AIRPAC) based at Naval Air Station Lemoore, California and one based at Marine Corps Air Station Iwakuni, Japan.

Carrier Air Wing 2

Currently USS *Carl Vinson* (CVN 70) has CVW-2 assigned and departed the United States in mid-November 2024 for a deployment to the 7th Fleet Indo-Pacific region.

On March 24, 2025, the Carl Vinson Carrier Strike Group (CVCSG) arrived in Guam for a scheduled port visit following involvement in exercises with the Republic of Korea Navy and the Japan Maritime Self-Defense Force. Seven days later the CVCSG departed Guam and set sail for the US Central Command (CENTCOM)

area of responsibility (AOR), following an order issued by Secretary of Defense (SECDF) Pete Hegseth for two carriers to be in CENTCOM during April. The order was issued to support an increase in the number of air strikes on the Yemen-based Houthi rebels. The second carrier deployed was USS *Nimitz* (CVN 68). By early July, the two carriers were underway in the US 5th Fleet.

After leaving the 5th Fleet area, the USS *Carl Vinson* was underway in the Philippine Sea on its return transit to its home port of San Diego. Flight operations involved F/A-18 Super Hornet and F-35C Lightning II fighters for many mission sets held by an air wing which include precision strike, air and missile defence, anti-submarine

CARRIER AIR WING 2 SQUADRONS

HSC-4	MH-60S	Black Knights
HSM-78	MH-60R	Blue Hawks
VAQ-136	EA-18G	Gauntlets
VAW-113	E-2D AR	Black Eagles
VFA-2	F/A-18F	Bounty Hunters
VFA-113	F/A-18E	Stingers
VFA-97	F-35C	Warhawks
VFA-192	F/A-18E	Golden Dragons
VRM-30 Det 1	CMV-22B	Titans

warfare, and what's known as sea control, ensuring that the US and its allies can use the sea for their purposes and denying its use to adversaries. Execution of the mission sets in the Philippine Sea is significant for the protection of freedom of navigation along trade routes in the face of China's territorial claims in the region.

Carrier Air Wing 5

Based at Marine Corps Air Station Iwakuni, Japan, CVW-5 had a busy 2024. It departed Japan embarked on USS *Ronald Reagan* (CVN 76) in May 2024, sailed to San Diego and subsequently completed a hull swap with USS *George Washington* (CVN 73). *Reagan* was the USN's forward-deployed carrier, meaning it was permanently based at Fleet Activities Yokosuka, Japan, since 2015.

During its time in the United States, CVW-5's squadrons undertook an Air Wing Fallon detachment at the desert base in northern Nevada. During its time in the United States over the late summer of 2024, CVW-5 re-equipped with three new aircraft types to upgrade its configuration to an Air Wing of the Future. F-35C-equipped VFA-147 joined CVW-5 replacing the F/A-18E-equipped VFA-115. CVW-5's airborne command and control squadron VAW-125 transitioned to E-2D aircraft equipped with aerial refuelling probes, and its carrier onboard delivery tasking changed from the C-2A greyhound-equipped VRC-40 Det 5 to the brand new CMV-22B Osprey operated by VRM-30 Det 5.

According to the Navy League's *Sea Power* magazine: "The *George Washington* with CVW-7 embarked departed Norfolk on April 25, 2024, and completed a series of US Southern Command exercises with Argentina, Brazil, Chile, Colombia, Ecuador, Peru, and Uruguay, and conducted port visits planned for Brazil, Chile, and Peru. USS *George Washington* arrived at Naval Air Station North Island, California, on July 10, 2024, after its round-the horn voyage from Norfolk, Virginia."

Commenting on the air wing's new configuration upon its return to Japan, commander of the George Washington Carrier Strike Group, Rear Admiral Greg Newkirk said: "Carrier Air Wing 5 represents the Navy's determined investments in naval aviation through cutting-edge technology and our most advanced training with years of unmatched experience flying in this consequential theatre. Our forward-deployed forces in Japan are among our most capable in the world and represent a tangible sign of America's commitment to Japan and the region."

On June 10, 2025, USS *George Washington* left Yokosuka on its first deployment since it returned to Japan the previous November. Between May 19-31, the squadrons operating fixed wing types assigned to CVW-5 completed field carrier-landing practice (FCLP) at Iwo To on the island of Iwo Jima. FCLP is a required flight training event for pilot qualification and proficiency that precedes aircraft carrier landing operations.

Discussing the FCLP requirement in a release, Captain William Fallon, assistant chief of staff for Commander, US Naval Forces Japan said: "There is a great amount of effort in the practice and the professionalism that goes into learning how to do this. The carrier environment is very challenging to work in—whether it's daytime or night-time. A large carrier suddenly feels very small when you do it, so it's incumbent on us to practice

Below: **An EA-18G Growler, assigned to Electronic Attack Squadron 142 launches from the flight deck of the world's largest aircraft carrier, USS Gerald R. Ford.** USN/MC2 Tajh Payne

realistically as we found right here, which is the benefit of Iwo To. It's very dark at night, so it feels similar to the carrier environment."

The FCLPs also provided valuable training to CVW-5's landing signal officers (LSO), dubbed paddles, naval aviators specifically trained to guide and ensure the safe recovery of aircraft aboard aircraft carriers.

Explaining the FCLP training, Lieutenant Commander Tory West, an LSO attached to CVW-5 said: "Today, specifically, the paddles are training on the manually operated visual landing aid system [MOVLAS]. The pilots must respond to the MOVLAS system differently, so if the ship is moving differently, the pilots can adjust and land safely."

Although the facility at Iwo To offers an invaluable training opportunity for fixed-wing pilots and aircrew, it is not suitable as a permanent FCLP site due

to difficulty in maintaining its remote facilities and lack of optional diversion airfields for use during inclement weather or other situations. According to the USN release, the US government reserves the right to conduct FCLP at mainland facilities when required.

Discussing the challenges of the Iwo To site, Fallon said: "One of the challenges of operating out of Iwo To is we don't have the ability to divert an aircraft somewhere else, if there is an emergency; if there is bad weather, or something happens in the air. So, if there's a problem, we don't have any other place to land whereas if we had an area to conduct FCLPs much closer to land, it would provide much bigger safety margins for us to operate and train."

CARRIER AIR WING 5 SQUADRONS

HSC-12	MH-60S	Golden Falcons
HSM-77	MH-60R	Saberhawks
VAQ-141	EA-18G	Shadowhawks
VAW-125	E-2D AR	Tigertails
VFA-27	F/A-18E	Royal Maces
VFA-102	F/A-18F	Diamondbacks
VFA-147	F-35C	Argonauts
VFA-195	F/A-18E	Dambusters
VRM-30 Det 5	CMV-22B	Titans

Below: **An aviation boatswain's mate assigned to the air department aboard the USS *Gerald R. Ford*, signals an E-2D Hawkeye assigned to Airborne Command and Control Squadron 124 on the flight deck.** USN/MC2 Jacob Mattingly

The People's Liberation Army Navy (PLAN) increased activity in the South China Sea region at the time that USS *George Washington* set sail. According to Japan's Joint Staff, the PLAN carrier *Liaoning* and its accompanying warships entered the easternmost sector of Japan's exclusive economic zone. The PLAN carrier *Shandong* was also underway with four accompanying warships to the southeast of Okinawa's Miyako Island. According to Japan's Ministry of Defense, this was the first occasion that both of China's active carriers had been underway simultaneously in the Pacific.

George Washington and the associated warships in the GWCSG departed anchorage at Manila, Philippines, on July 7, 2025, after a scheduled four-day port visit to continue their transit to the Timor Sea to participate in Exercise Talisman Sabre 2025.

Above: **An MH-60S Seahawk, assigned to Helicopter Sea Combat Squadron 6, takes off from the flight deck of the USS *Nimitz* during flight operations in the US Central Command area of responsibility.** USN

The GWCSG met up and conducted dual carrier operations with the HMS *Prince of Wales*, deployed under Operation Highmast, making this year's edition of Talisman Sabre the first to involve a US and British carrier since the exercise began in 2005. The dual ops were the first conducted by the GWCSG since it returned to Japan in 2024.

On July 18, the USS *George Washington* was underway in with USS *America*, HMS *Prince of Wales*, and JS *Kaga* at the start of Exercise Pacific Arsenal. Notably, three of the carriers had a squadron of F-35s embarked, in the future the *JS Kaga* will embark F-35Bs. The exercise was staged in response to China's military build-up in the region.

Carrier Air Wing 9

In October 2023, the USS *Abraham Lincoln* (CVN 72) completed a major maintenance period known as Planned Incremental Availability during which critical equipment is repaired, new systems are installed, and configuration upgrades designed to help maintain the ship's operational readiness.

On July 11, 2024, USS *Abraham Lincoln* left Naval Air Station North Island in San Diego and set sail for the CENTCOM AOR where it arrived on August 20. The Abraham Carrier Strike Group included the embarked CVW-9 and its associated warships, all of which joined the US-led Operation Prosperity Guardian designed to protect merchant shipping in the region.

The ABECSG's transit to the 5th Fleet/ CENTCOM AOR was accelerated under an order issued by then Secretary of Defense (SECDEF) Lloyd Austin following heightened tension with Iran and its proxy armed groups.

USS *Abraham Lincoln* sailed through the Strait of Malacca on August 27, bound for the Indian Ocean and the US 5th Fleet area. The 104,000-ton ship was due to relieve the USS *Theodore Roosevelt* (CVN 71), which had been operating in the 5th Fleet area in support of Operation Prosperity Guardian since June. But the *Roosevelt* remained on station as ordered by the SECDEF on September 29, six days after its replacement, the USS *Harry S Truman* (CVN 75) left Norfolk, Virginia on September 23.

While the Lincoln was on deployment, Naval Air Systems Command issued a press release stating that aviators assigned to CVW-9 could train onboard the ship using advanced simulators developed and installed by the Naval Air Warfare Center Aircraft Division (NAWCAD).

The first-of-a-kind training capability, called Simulators at Sea, features connected desktop trainers that enable aviators to practice missions together while deployed - a historically limited capability.

Aviators assigned to CVW-9 were the first to rehearse naval missions including wartime scenarios with Simulators at Sea. Previously, joint mission training on this scale was significantly limited because practicing wartime scenarios holds risk, flight operations can be expensive, and open-air rehearsal puts USN tactics on display for adversaries.

Simulators at Sea was implemented in less than 12 months following lessons learned from the 2023 deployment of NAWCAD F-35 simulators onboard USS *Carl Vinson*, which has greater complexity and required significant integration efforts from organisations across the Naval Aviation Enterprise.

Perhaps in anticipation of a growing likelihood of combat ops in the 5th Fleet area, NAWCAD accelerated production and delivery of a mission data file (MDF) for the F-35C aircraft assigned to Marine Fighter Attack Squadron 314 (VMFA-314), one of CVW-9's strike fighter squadrons.

A team from NAWCAD provided the essential MDF which included the latest intelligence updates and design enhancements that enable pilots to identify and counter threats in specific operational environments. The update incorporated more than 100 intelligence changes and multiple design improvements, significantly enhancing the aircraft's survivability and lethality.

There was some smart thinking about the updated MDF because VMFA-314 conducted the first air strikes for the F-35C aircraft on November 9-10 against weapons storage facilities in Yemen, those controlled by the Houthis and most likely used to target military and civilian vessels navigating international waters in the Red Sea and Gulf of Aden. According to the USN, the facilities struck housed conventional weapons, including anti-ship missiles.

Commenting in a release on the strikes, Lieutenant Colonel Jeffrey Davis, commanding officer of VMFA-314, said: "The F-35C demonstrated its warfighting advantage by transiting contested airspace and striking targets in the heart of Houthi territory over multiple days."

Also commenting, CVW-9's commander, Captain Gerald Tritz said: "The offensive and defensive capabilities of the F-35C absolutely enhance our air wing's striking arm. The now battle-tested Air Wing of the Future has proven itself a game changer across all carrier air wing missions."

As a note, the F-35B first saw combat in 2018 when units assigned to the Essex Amphibious Ready Group conducted airstrikes against the Taliban in Afghanistan and ISIS in Syria, and the F-35A completed that variant's first combat missions flown against ISIS targets in Iraq during 2019.

When the USS *Abraham Lincoln* left the Red Sea over the weekend of November 16-17, a three-month deployment ended and left the 5th Fleet without a CSG for the second time in over a year. The carrier's withdrawal from the 5th Fleet area was announced one week after two major Houthi military operations against US warships in the Red Sea. CENTCOM officials later said nobody was injured, and no warships were damaged in the attack. Eight attack drones, five anti-ship ballistic missiles, and four anti-ship cruise missiles were reportedly shot down.

The ABECSG returned to San Diego on December 20, 2024, at the end of a five-month deployment which included several firsts as highlighted in a release by Commander, Carrier Strike Group 3, Rear Admiral Adan Cruz who said: "Our incredibly successful deployment of firsts included the first combat employment of the F-35C Lightning II platform, the first employment of the ALQ-249 Next Generation Jammer, the first Nimitz-class aircraft carrier to refuel at sea with a commercial oiler, the first multi-large deck event with the Italian Navy's Cavour CSG in the Indo-Pacific, the first west coast CSG to conduct combat strikes to degrade Iranian-backed Houthi rebel combat capabilities, and the first carrier to pull into Malaysia in over 12 years to strengthen critical regional partnerships."

Above: **An EA-18G Growler, assigned to Electronic Attack Squadron 139, launches from the flight deck of the USS *Nimitz* during flight operations in the US Central Command area of responsibility.** USN

EA-18G Growlers assigned to Electronic Attack Squadron 133 (VAQ-133) both deployed and employed the ALQ-249 for the first time including in combat providing a previously unmatched electronic warfare capability.

CVW-9 flew over 9,000 sorties and amassed over 21,000 flight hours. USS *Abraham Lincoln* undertook 28 replenishments-at-sea and travelled for more than 78,000nm, and the ships of the ABECSG conducted routine port visits in Egypt, Guam, Malaysia, Pakistan, Saipan, Singapore, Sri Lanka, and Thailand.

Carrier Air Wing 11

Following its departure from Naval Air Station North Island, California on January 11, 2024, USS *Theodore Roosevelt*

CARRIER AIR WING 9 SQUADRONS

HSC-14	MH-60S	Chargers
HSM-71	MH-60R	Raptors
VAQ-133	EA-18G	Wizards
VAW-117	E-2D AR	Wallbangers
VFA-14	F/A-18E	Tophatters
VFA-41	F/A-18E	Black Aces
VFA-151	F/A-18E	Vigilantes
VMFA-314	F-35C	Black Knights
VRC-40 Det 1	C-2A	Rawhides

embarked CVW-11 and sailed west across the Pacific.

On January 31, while underway in the Philippine Sea the TRCSG, the USS Carl Vinson CSG and the Japan Maritime Self-Defense Force (JMSDF) conducted a Multi-Large Deck Event (MLDE).

The MLDE provided USN and JMSDF ships and assigned aircraft an opportunity to conduct air defence drills, sea surveillance, cross-deck exercises, and tactical manoeuvres training to advance unique high-end warfighting capabilities.

Commenting on the MLDE, Rear Admiral Carlos Sardiello, commander, Carrier Strike Group 1 (CSG-1) said: The US and Japan are capable of rapidly assembling multiple large-deck naval forces in support of mutual security interests in the Indo

Pacific. Our ability to rapidly aggregate and work collectively alongside the JMSDF and the Theodore Roosevelt strike group is positive proof."

Both CSG-1 and CSG-9 are made up of a multiplatform team of ships and aircraft, capable of carrying out a wide variety of missions. Assets from CSG-1 involved in the MLDE comprised CVW-2, Ticonderoga class guided-missile cruiser USS Princeton (CG 59), Arleigh Burke-class guided-missile destroyers USS Sterett (DDG 104), USS Dewey (DDG 105), USS Rafael Peralta (DDG 115), and USS John Finn (DDG 113).

Assets from CSG-9 involved were CVW-11, guided-missile cruiser USS Lake Erie (CG 70), and three Arleigh Burke-class guided-missile destroyers, USS William P. Lawrence (DDG 110), USS Daniel K. Inouye

(DDG 118) and USS Halsey (DDG 97). The Japanese Maritime Self Defense Force's deployed the Hyuga-class helicopter destroyer JS Ise (DDH 182).

On March 19, while underway in the South China Sea, the USS Theodore Roosevelt completed its 250,000th successful arrested landing. Commander Brandon Miller, CVW-11's operations officer landed an F/A-18F Super Hornet during routine operations in the South China Sea: the event took place nearly 38 years after the Roosevelt first deployed with an air wing embarked.

Following a port visit to Busan, Republic of Korea, the Theodore Roosevelt Carrier Strike Group (TRCSG) sailed to participate in Exercise Freedom Edge, the inaugural US-Republic of Korea-Japan

Above: **Sailors conduct flight operations on the flight deck of the USS Carl Vinson on July 22, 2025, while underway in the 7th Fleet area of operations.** USN/MC Seaman Apprentice Pablo Chavez

multi-domain exercise held in the Sea of Japan between June 27-29. In addition to the aircraft assigned to CVW-11, the USN also deployed P-8A Poseidon maritime patrol aircraft.

The exercise trained for interoperability between the three nations with the political objective of creating stability in the Indo-Pacific area, including the Korean Peninsula. It involved co-operative ballistic missile defence, air defence, anti-submarine warfare, search and rescue, and maritime interdiction.

Japanese and Korean warships and aircraft involved were the JMSDF destroyer helicopter carrier JS *Ise* (DDH-182), destroyer JS *Atago* (DDG-177) and a P-1 MPA. The Republic of Korea Navy

had two destroyers involved, the ROKS *Seoae-Ryu-Seong-ryong* (DDG-993) and the ROKS *Gang Gam-Chan* (DDG-979), a Lynx helicopter, and a P-3C Orion MPA. The Republic of Korea Air Force participated with F-16 Falcons, likely conducting maritime strike missions.

In June, the TRCSG joined with the USS Ronald Reagan CSG to drill together during Exercise Valiant Shield between June 7-18 on Guam, the Commonwealth of the Northern Mariana Islands, Palau, and at sea around the Mariana Island Range Complex.

Valiant Shield is a multinational, biennial field training exercise focused on interoperability in a multi-domain environment. The exercise prepares the

CARRIER AIR WING 11 SQUADRONS

HSC-8	MH-60S	Eightballers
HSM-75	MH-60R	Wolf Pack
VAQ-137	EA-18G	Rooks
VAW-115	E-2D AR	Liberty Bells
VFA-25	F/A-18E	Fist of Fleets
VFA-86	F-35C	Sidewinders
VFA-154	F/A-18F	Black Knights
VFA-211	F/A-18E	Fighting Checkmates
VRC-40 Det	C-2A	Rawhides

Joint and Combined Force to rapidly respond to crises and contingencies across a spectrum of operations from humanitarian assistance and disaster relief to armed conflict.

The TRCSG was bound for the 5th Fleet area where it arrived on July 12 to conduct maritime security operations.

During routine operations on August 23, a rigid inflatable boat (RIB) from the Arleigh Burke-class guided-missile destroyer

USS *Daniel Inouye* (DDG 118) and an MH-60S search and rescue (SAR) helicopter from CVW-9's HSC-8 successfully recovered two mariners from the water and flown to the carrier for medical care.

After leaving the 5th Fleet area on September 12, the TRCSG sailed through the 7th Fleet and 3rd Fleet areas and onward to Naval Air Station North Island where it arrived on October 15 completing 278 days underway.

Carrier Air Wing 17

The USS *Nimitz* departed Naval Base Kitsap in Bremerton, Washington, on March 21, 2025, for a scheduled deployment

CARRIER AIR WING 17 SQUADRONS

HSC-6	MH-60S	Indians
HSM-73	MH-60R	Battle Cats
VAQ-139	EA-18G	Cougars
VAW-121	E-2D AR	Bluetails
VFA-22	F/A-18F	Fighting Redcocks
VFA-94	F/A-18E	Mighty Shrieks
VFA-137	F/A-18E	Kestrels
VFA-146	F/A-18E	Blue Diamonds
VRC-40 Det	C-2A	Rawhides

to the Western Pacific. Its first stop, on March 24, was Naval Air Station North Island in San Diego where it remained for two days before getting underway on March 26, heading out to the eastern Pacific operating area where CVW-17 flew onboard.

Nimitz and two of the warships in the NIMCSG, destroyers USS *Gridley* (DDG 101) and USS *Lenah Sutcliffe Higbee* (DDG 123) made a port visit to Guam during the third week of April.

In a news release, the USN said: "The Nimitz Carrier Strike Group's port visit to Guam highlights the Navy's

ongoing commitment to maintaining a strong, forward presence in the Western Pacific. Positioned in a region of increasing strategic importance, the strike group plays a critical role in deterring aggression and upholding regional stability. Operating from Guam enhances the Navy's ability to protect vital supply routes and infrastructure, while deepening coordination with allies and partners."

After conducting routine operations in the South China Sea, the NIMCSG sailed through the Strait of Malacca bound for the 5th Fleet area.

Below: **The Nimitz-class aircraft carrier USS *Carl Vinson* underway in the South China Sea, on July 18, 2025.** USN/MC Seaman Apprentice Matthew Green

The final four CVWs listed are those assigned to Commander, Naval Air Forces Atlantic (AIRLANT) based at Naval Air Station Oceana, Virginia.

Carrier Air Wing 1

USS Harry S Truman CSG (HSTSG) arrived in the Red Sea on December 14, 2024, with CVW-1 embarked. The HSTSG was tasked with providing combat support against Iran-backed Houthi rebels in Yemen following the group's missile and drone strikes against commercial ships and military warships that started in November 2023.

On March 16, 2024, Fox News correspondent Lucas Tomlinson reported on X that a senior US official had confirmed that US warships had shot down about a dozen Houthi drones targeting the Truman strike group since the US airstrikes that night. The drones were shot down well before they posed a serious threat.

Those strikes were conducted in response to the Houthis attempt to resume attacks on Israeli ships in the Red Sea and Gulf of Aden.

The March 15 strike was the first of CENTCOM's Operation Rough Rider, a sustained campaign against Houthi facilities and camps in Yemen. By April 29, CENTCOM forces had struck more than 1,000 targets including, according to CENTCOM, command-and-control facilities, air defence systems, advanced weapons manufacturing facilities, and

Below: Sailors conduct pre-flight checks on an F-35C Lightning II, assigned to Strike Fighter Squadron 97, on the flight deck of the USS *Carl Vinson* underway in the 7th Fleet area of operations. USN/MC Seaman Apprentice Pablo Chavez

weapons storage locations. CENTCOM claims the storage facilities housed anti-ship, ballistic and cruise missiles, unmanned aerial systems, and uncrewed surface vessels.

CENTCOM said Operation Rough Rider had degraded the pace and effectiveness of its attacks citing a 69% drop in ballistic missile launches and a 55% decrease in one-way drone attacks.

Aircraft assigned to the CVWs embarked on the USS *Harry S. Truman* and the USS *Carl Vinson* took part in the operations.

US officials told *The New York Times* that Houthi forces nearly shot down USAF F-16s and an F-35 within the first 30 days of Operation Rough Rider.

On May 5, The White House ordered an immediate halt to further missions based on a ceasefire mediated by Oman.

By the time Carrier Air Wing 1 left the Red Sea in early May 2025, it had launched more than 13,000 sorties, employed 770 weapons, dropped 1.1 million pounds of ordnance against more than 1,100 Houthi targets during a near two-month bombing campaign against Yemen's Houthi rebels.

Among the thousands of sorties launched from the *Truman*'s flight deck, one flown on February 1 was the largest-ever conducted against ISIS militants, not in Syria but the East African nation of Somalia. According to USN details released about the airstrike, 27 F/A-18 Super Hornets assigned to CVW-1 struck cave complexes used by and housing members of ISIS. The USN reckoned that 16 of the 27 Super Hornets launched dropped 124,000lb of ordnance in less than two minutes.

In a February 11 statement, US Africa Command stated: "The joint airstrikes targeted senior ISIS-Somalia leadership in

CARRIER AIR WING 1 SQUADRONS

HSC-11	MH-60S	Drago Slayers
HSM-72	MH-60R	Proud Warriors
VAQ-144	EA-18G	Main Battery
VAW-126	E-2D AR	Seahawks
VFA-11	F/A-18F	Red Rippers
VFA-81	F/A-18E	Sunliners
VFA-136	F/A-18E	Knight Hawks
VFA-143	F/A-18E	Pukin' Dogs
VRC-40 Det 1	C-2A	Rawhides

a series of cave complexes approximately 50 miles southeast of Bosaso."

Despite the combat achievements, CVW-1 lost three Super Hornets in different mishaps during its time underway in the Red Sea. In December an F/A-18 was shot down by the guided missile cruiser USS *Gettysburg* in a friendly fire incident. In April a second jet was lost overboard while being towed in the hangar bay, followed less than two weeks later by a third jet lost in a failed landing. Equally alarming was a collision with a merchant ship in the Mediterranean Sea near Port Said, Egypt on February 13.

Carrier Air Wing 3

USS *Dwight D Eisenhower* (CVN 69) left Naval Station Norfolk, Virginia on October 14, 2023, for a scheduled deployment to the 6th Fleet area to maintain a US naval presence in the Eastern Mediterranean Sea.

During its transit through the Mediterranean Sea, USS *Dwight D Eisenhower* conducted dual carrier ops with USS *Gerald R Ford*, a notable event but also because it was the first occasion when two USN carriers were underway in the Eastern Mediterranean.

But the *Ike* and its CSG did not remain in the Med as planned but passed through the Suez Canal into the Red Sea to join USS *Bataan* (LHD-5) and USS *Carter Hall* (LSD-50)

In the late evening of January 7, 2024, F/A-18 Super Hornets assigned to CVW-3 launched from the flight deck of USS *Dwight D Eisenhower* were involved with the shoot down of 18 one-way attack drones, two anti-ship cruise missiles and one anti-ship ballistic missile, while underway in the Red Sea. The Super Hornets were not solely responsible for all 21 munitions, some were knocked down by surface-to-air missiles launched from USN destroyers the USS *Laboon* (DDG-58), USS *Gravely* (DDG-107), USS *Mason* (DDG-87), and the Royal Navy's HMS *Diamond* (D34). Earlier shoot downs of drones and missiles by CVW-3 Super Hornets took place on December 26, the air wing's first engagement with the Houthis, and December 31, 2023.

Operation Poseidon Archer conducted on January 22, 2024, involved strikes on a further eight Houthi targets located in Yemen. Tomahawk Land Attack Missiles fired from USN warships, and munitions dropped by CVW-3 Super Hornets and RAF Typhoon FGR4s formed the barrage conducted in response to continued attacks on commercial shipping and warships in the Red Sea. The coalition of nations involved in the strike (see below) claim 30 attacks on vessels underway in the Red Sea had been launched in the previous two months.

Above: **An EA-18G Growler, assigned to Electronic Attack Squadron 139, launches from the flight deck of the USS *Nimitz* during flight operations in the US Central Command area of responsibility.**
USN

CARRIER AIR WING 3 SQUADRONS

HSC-7	MH-60S	Dusty Dogs
HSM-74	MH-60R	Swamp Foxes
VAQ-130	EA-18G	Zappers
VAW-123	E-2D AR	Screwtops
VFA-32	F/A-18F	Swordsmen
VFA-83	F/A-18E	Rampagers
VFA-105	F/A-18E	Gunslingers
VFA-131	F/A-18E	Wildcats
VRC-40 Det	C-2A	Rawhides

A joint statement by Australia, Bahrain, Canada, the Netherlands, the UK and the US read: "These precision strikes are intended to disrupt and degrade the capabilities that the Houthis use to threaten global trade and the lives of innocent mariners, and are in response to a series of illegal, dangerous, and destabilising Houthi actions since our coalition strikes on January 11, including anti-ship ballistic missile and unmanned aerial system attacks that struck two US-owned merchant vessels. Today's strike specifically targeted a Houthi underground storage site and locations associated with the Houthis' missile and air surveillance capabilities."

Describing the Houthi actions against US warships in the IKECSG prior to *Ike*'s return to Norfolk, Rear Admiral Kavon Hakimzadeh, the commander of Carrier Strike Group 2 said: "We were operating in a maritime area that was under the weapons range of the Iranian-backed militia for seven of those nine months. Along the way, we employed the combat capabilities of every ship in a strike group to the maximum extent, using a lot of weapons for the first time ever, and… we've had sailors deal with the stress of operating under some tense conditions for a sustained amount of time – for the first time since probably World War Two. The real stress came from the fact that the enemy got to decide when they wanted to shoot, so you certainly had to be vigilant against that every day."

In November, the Yemen-based Houthis began attacking commercial ships transiting the Red Sea. Ships that the Houthis believed were associated with Israel. The group vowed to continue attacking commercial ships until the cessation of Israel's bombardment of Gaza. A group of nations led by the United States commenced Operation Prosperity Guardian to protect commercial ships transiting the Red Sea and Gulf of Aden.

According to the USN, between November 2023 and June 2024 aircraft assigned to CVW-3 launched at least 80 air-to-air missiles and 350 air-to-surface weapons against Houthi targets in Yemen, and the warships in the IKECSG launched more than 100 Tomahawk and Standard missiles.

After a nine-month deployment, USS *Dwight D. Eisenhower* returned to Naval Station Norfolk in July 2024. On January 14, 2025, the 101,000-ton ship arrived at Norfolk Naval Shipyard to commence a scheduled Planned Incremental Availability (PIA) period. A PIA is a shorter maintenance period compared to a major Refueling and Complex Overhaul.

PIA periods focus on specific system upgrades and routine repairs. The *Ike*'s PIA includes comprehensive work on the carrier's propulsion systems, crew berths, combat, and aviation support systems, all designed to ensure the ship's long-term mission readiness.

Above: **An F-35C Lightning II, assigned to Strike Fighter Squadron 97, launches from the flight deck of the USS *Carl Vinson* in the US Central Command area of responsibility.** USN

Carrier Air Wing 7

The USS *George HW Bush* (CVN 77) was the only carrier assigned to TBC that did not deploy to the 6th and 5th Fleet areas. The ship went through a ten-month PIA between July 29, 2023, and April 2024. During its PIA the *Bush* underwent upgrades of its navigation, communications, weapons, and combat control systems. Follow-on sea trials tested all the upgraded systems and included assessments of systems that ensure operational readiness, not least propulsion and power generation.

Because of the *Bush*'s PIA, CVW-7, its assigned air wing has not deployed but continued shore-based training ahead of returning to sea aboard the Bush in 2026.

Carrier Air Wing 8

America's newest aircraft carrier and the world's largest warship, the first-in-class USS Gerald R Ford, returned to Naval Station Norfolk on January 17, 2024, after a deployment to 6th Fleet area and three extensions ordered by the then SECDEF Lloyd Austin.

Sailing from Norfolk on May 2, 2023, the Ford and its CSG sailed to the North Sea and Baltic Seas to participate in various NATO exercises. Following a port call to Oslo, the GFCSG sailed to the Mediterranean where it remained underway for several months, including the sector close to Israel brought about by the October 7 Hamas attack on southern Israel.

According to a USN release: "In total, the GRFCSG worked with 17 nations throughout its deployment during exercises Baltic Operations, Air Defender, a Bomber Task Force, Viking Trident, Neptune Strike, and Sage Wolverine. The strike group operated with Standing NATO Maritime Groups 1 and 2, conducted dual-carrier operations with USS Dwight D Eisenhower (CVN 69), and exercised with navies from France, Greece, Norway, Türkiye, and the United Kingdom."

Ford's three deployment extensions were ordered in mid-October after the Hamas attack on southern Israel, November and December caused by the Houthi drone and missile attacks on ships transiting the Red Sea. The USN said the *Ford* was deployed for 239 days, conducted 33,444 flight deck moves, 3,124 hangar bay aircraft moves, 2,883 aircraft elevator moves, 16,351 aircraft fuelling evolutions, and transferred 8,850 pallets of cargo and mail.

From the crew's perspective, the ship's culinary team prepared and served 3.1 million meals, which included approximately 48,000 dozen eggs, 24,000 gallons of milk, 131,000 hamburgers, 367,000lb of chicken, and 79,000 chocolate chip cookies.

As an indicator of how stretched the USN's aircraft carrier fleet is, the *Ford* set

CARRIER AIR WING 7 SQUADRONS

HSC-5	MH-60S	Night Dippers
HSM-46	MH-60R	Griffins
VAQ-140	EA-18G	Patriots
VAW-116	E-2C NP	Sun Kings
VFA-103	F/A-18F	Jolly Rogers
VRC-40 Det	C-2A	Rawhides

Below: **Sailors conduct pre-flight safety checks on an F-35C Lightning II, assigned to Strike Fighter Squadron 97, on the flight deck of the USS *Carl Vinson* in the US Central Command area of responsibility.** USN

CARRIER AIR WING 8 SQUADRONS

HSC-9	MH-60S	Tridents
HSM-70	MH-60R	Spartans
VAQ-142	EA-18G	Gray Wolves
VAW-124	E-2D AR	Bear Aces
VFA-31	F/A-18E	Tomcatters
VFA-37	F/A-18E	Bulls
VFA-87	F/A-18E	Golden Warriors
VFA-213	F/A-18F	Black Lions
VRC-40 Det	C-2A	Rawhides

Right: **An F/A-18E Super Hornet, assigned to Strike Fighter Squadron 195, takes off from the flight deck of USS *George Washington* (CVN 73) while underway in the Timor Sea, during Exercise Talisman Sabre on July 15, 2025.** USN/MC Seaman Nicolas Quezada

sail from Naval Station Norfolk for its second deployment on June 24, 2025.

Speaking to the press prior to the *Ford*'s departure from Norfolk, Captain David Dartez, commander, Carrier Air Wing 8 said: "Over the last two weeks since the *Truman* got back, I have had multiple meetings with the commander of Carrier Air Wing 1. We went over everything, every little detail, what our adversaries are doing, how we counter that. And the grand picture of reliance, quality of life for sailors."

On July 21, the GRFCSG was underway in the Mediterranean Sea.

Training Carrier Air Wings

Each USN carrier air wing comprises a similar complement of aircraft types assigned, though some now include the F-35C and F/A-18 Super Hornet. Prior to deploying an air wing, each of its squadrons undergoes a training programme that culminates with two major training events: Air Wing Fallon ashore at Naval Air Station Fallon, involving the entire wing, and COMPTUEX (Composite Training Unit Exercise) involving the entire carrier strike group at sea.

For much of the air wing's work-up period, each squadron follows a unit-level advanced readiness programme implemented by the appropriate weapons school. The different programs are listed in the table below.

SFARP

Based on the number of strike fighters assigned to each air wing, by far the largest of the programs is the Strike Fighter Advanced Readiness Program (SFARP). Rated as a unit-level training programme, SFARP is intended to maximise the tactical proficiency of strike fighter aircrews across the full spectrum of F/A-18 and F-35C mission sets by using academic lectures, simulator events, and tactical training sorties.

SFARP is divided into segments starting with one dedicated to the air-to-surface mission set which comprises academic lectures and simulator events designed to baseline all F/A-18 aircrew with their type's current OFP (Operational Flight Program) software and its functionality. All simulator events are given and evaluated by strike fighter tactics instructors from the weapon school.

An instructor pilot grades and monitors everything the aircrew does in the simulator including an instructor weapon system officer (WSO) if the crew flies the two-seat F/A-18F. The aircrew (not the instructors) brief, execute and debrief the event. The instructors are present throughout and break down the entire event during the debrief. Instructors scrutinise every action the aircrew

US NAVAL AVIATION ADVANCE READINESS PROGRAMS

Program name	Type	Weapon School
EWARP Electronic Warfare Advanced Readiness Program	EA-18G	Electronic Attack Weapons School, based at Naval Air Station Whidbey Island, Washington
CARP COD Advanced Readiness Program	C-2A Greyhound and CMV-22B Osprey	Airborne Command & Control and Logistics Weapons School (ACCLWS) based at Naval Air Station Norfolk, Virginia with a detachment located at Naval Base Ventura County Point Mugu, California
HARP Helicopter Advanced Readiness Program	MH-60R Seahawk	Helicopter Maritime Strike Weapons School Atlantic and Pacific based at Naval Air Station Jacksonville, Florida, and Naval Air Station North Island respectively.
HARP Helicopter Advanced Readiness Program	MH-60S Seahawk	Helicopter Sea Combat Weapons School Atlantic and Pacific based at Naval Air Station Norfolk, Virginia and Naval Air Station North Island, California respectively
HARP Hawkeye Advanced Readiness Program	E-2C Hawkeye and E-2D Advanced Hawkeye	Airborne Command & Control and Logistics Weapons School (ACCLWS) based at Naval Air Station Norfolk, Virginia with a detachment located at Naval Base Ventura County Point Mugu, California
SFARP Strike Fighter Advanced Readiness Program	F/A-18 Super Hornet and F-35C Lightning II	Strike Fighter Weapons School Atlantic and Pacific based at Naval Air Station Ocean, Virginia and Naval Air Station Lemoore, California respectively.

take, including their use of the aircraft's software and whether they collected battle damage assessment as they came off the target. It's a 'start to finish' of exactly what they should do during the sims.

Post-simulators, the Super Hornet squadrons deploy to Naval Air Station Fallon, where aircrews drop inert and live munitions on the Fallon Range Training Complex to complete the air-to-surface segment of SFARP.

The air-to-surface segment focuses on training aircrew to employ weapons effectively and accurately – weapons such as the precision-guided Joint Direct Attack Munition-series and air-to-surface missiles.

SFARP air-to-surface segment aims to enhance tactical proficiency and ensure aircrews are ready for any contingency in their assigned area of operations, while emphasising continuous improvement and refinement of air-to-surface tactics and techniques.

Next up is the air-to-air segment which, like the air-to-surface segment, starts with academic lectures followed by simulators. During missions, Super Hornet squadrons and aircrews fly against heavy threat laydowns, the term used for the array of surface-to-air, air-to-air, and electronic warfare threats, comprising lots of adversary aircraft which are prosecuted either by interception to identify them or by shooting them down at range.

The air-to-air segment emphasises dogfighting, missile employment, and other aerial combat tactics.

All missions are flown in scenarios which are designed to mimic real-world threats and operational environments, pushing the pilots and WSOs to their limits. Presented with adversary aircraft,

Left: **Sailors prepare to launch an E-2D Hawkeye, assigned to Airborne Command and Control Squadron 115, off the flight deck of the USS *Theodore Roosevelt* on July 25, 2025, underway in the 3rd Fleet area of operations.** USN/ MC 3C Aaron Haro Gonzalez

Above: **One of six F-35C Lightning II aircraft assigned to Strike Fighter Squadron 147 (VFA-147) operating with the USS Carl Vinson (CVN 70), launches from the flight deck while underway in the Philippine Sea, on December 13, 2024.** USN/MC3 Nate Jordan

to Fallon to use the extensive range to execute the latest tactics, techniques, and procedures instructed by the Electronic Attack Weapons School, based at Naval Air Station Whidbey Island, Washington, to baseline the squadron's training with that of its seven sister squadrons. All air wing aircrew start the work-up cycle with the same baseline level of training, which functions as a levelling function that gets each aviator spun up on the latest TTPs.

Trapping

Landing on an aircraft carrier is a physical process. It involves catching one of the landing wires laid out across the aft of the area designated and marked for landing, the process is dubbed a trap. Damage is sometimes inflicted on the aircraft, or the jolt causes an issue such that the aircraft is side-lined. In lots of cases, the maintenance department can fix, refuel, and rearm the aircraft for its next mission. Compared to a Nimitz-class carrier, the process of refuelling, rearming, and relaunching an aircraft is a much faster

and more efficient process on the USS *Gerald R Ford*. The bigger flight deck and the island positioned further aft, provide more room to stage aircraft, position them for the catapults ready to launch. A key enabler is the method for refuelling, rearming and relaunching aircraft.

Precision Landing Mode

Today, recovering aircraft to a flight deck is aided by a ship-to-aircraft system called precision landing mode (PLM). Its full programme name is a bit of a tongue twister – the Maritime Augmented Guidance with Integrated Controls for Carrier Approach and Recovery Precision Enabling Technologies – or MAGIC CARPET, development of which started in 2016.

Functioning with optimised control laws and tailored displays, PLM significantly reduces the pilot's workload and the number of control inputs required during the last 17 seconds of final approach when task saturation is its highest. According to NAVAIR's PMA-265, PLM also improves overall flight cycle recovery time,

reduces the need for tanker aircraft and streamlines training requirements.

PLM was first delivered to fleet squadrons in October 2020 and continues to function under aircraft system failure conditions, most notably a single-engine approach. With one engine inoperable, PLM makes subtle control inputs that aid the aircraft's control during the final approach such that it stays in balanced flight.

For the pilot, a PLM-assisted approach feels like an approach flown with both engines operable, and there are very few situations that an aircraft cannot be brought aboard in PLM mode.

A single engine aircraft or one with a flight control problem coming in can be safely recovered. The PLM makes compensating inputs. PLM is critical and really earns its money when a bad sea state is in effect, which PLM can compensate for.

The computer can anticipate what the pilot is doing, compensate for wind and sea state, make super fine adjustments to

Prior to flying aboard, new pilots fly field carrier landing practice approaches (FCLPs) at an outlying field with a full-size flight deck layout marked on the runway. They must pass that event to get to the ship. When they fly to the ship, they use PLM, the mode takes a half a second to set, after which they make manual corrections and listen to the LSO to make immediate adjustments based on their instructions. This is done for safety because the LSO uses systems that the pilot doesn't have on the aircraft. The LSO tells the pilot if they are right of course, despite what the pilot is seeing; if they're a little low, a little high, the LSO tells the pilot to adjust their aircraft, and to immediately react.

Today, new pilots land aboard having never flown a manual pass, because they don't have to fly manual passes under any safety circumstances, because the PLM system is so reliable.

Data Exchange

By no means a new capability, Link-16, enables data to be exchanged between every platform in the entire air wing. If an aircraft or helicopter can beam information up to the E-2D – which coordinates everything for the mission with better line-of-sight connectivity – the E-2D can co-ordinate, for example, a strike against the target by linking the information to F/A-18s.

The E-2D is equipped with the Co-operative Engagement Capability (CEC) system which, according to official USN documents, makes it possible for multiple surface ships and aircraft to form an air defence network for the purpose of sharing radar target measurements in real time. The ability to share data from all capable sensors in a battle force provides increased timeliness, accuracy, and continuity for greater engagement decision and prosecution responsiveness.

According to official Navy documentation, the CEC system provides a sensor network with integrated fire control capability that significantly improves battle force air and missile defence capabilities by co-ordinating measurement data from air search sensors on CEC-equipped units into a single, integrated real-time, composite track air picture. The CEC sensor netting system extracts sensor-derived information and distributes a superset of the best anti-air warfare sensor data to all CEC co-operating units (CUs) participating in carrier strike groups. Each CU independently employs high capacity, parallel processing, and advanced algorithms to combine all distributed sensor data into a fire control quality track picture improving its own unit track precision, consistency, and continuity which expands detection range and increases reaction time. CEC also provides situational awareness by enabling longer range, co-operative, multiple, or layered engagement strategies to improve strike force effectiveness and is highly resistant to jamming and delivers accurate gridlocking between CUs.

As data is exchanged, all aircraft and helicopter aircrews receive the target information which they can enter in their targeting system, to prosecute the target increasing situational awareness for everyone, and is a force multiplier. If an MH-60R has visually spotted a submarine's periscope, or has detected something with its sensor systems, that information can be shared across a broad network of assets, including a P-8A Poseidon, to help quickly prosecute the target.

the aircraft, and maintain the glide slope all the way to the deck. It increases the safety margin significantly.

Despite PLM, landing signal officers (LSOs) still work from a platform at the aft of the ship to retain a 'man in the loop' to assist getting pilots aboard which is critical. LSOs provide a final safety check and tell the pilot to make fine adjustments to safely get aboard, even with PLM.

PLM makes a significant difference on the final approach phase of flight; it's a game changer, especially when things aren't going well, and the pilot is relying on instruments to land aboard.

New pilots for the F/A-18 Super Hornet and EA-18G Growler use PLM from day one of their training, and carrier air wing squadrons use PLM for carrier qualifications which reduces their training requirements by up to 50%.

Commander, Naval Air Force has authorised new pilots with the two Super Hornet fleet replacement squadrons to use PLM when flying aboard an aircraft carrier for the first time.

Below: **Sailors direct an F-35C Lightning II assigned to Strike Fighter Squadron 97 across the flight deck of the USS *Carl Vinson* in the US Central Command area of responsibility.** USN

NAVAIR determined the profiles and optimum closure rates that work best for the E-2D aircraft, metrics that are important for the pilot to avoid hitting the aerial refuelling basket too hard because the closure rate is too fast, causing a sine wave in the hose which comes back to the E-2D and may rip off the probe. The probe has a control break-off point above which it will disconnect from the hose to prevent damage to either the F/A-18 tanker or the E-2D.

Air Wing Fallon

Air Wing Fallon is the capstone event of an air wing's work-up and involves all eight squadrons operating at the peak level of their capability. Conducted at Naval Air Station Fallon, the training here includes include mission planning, execution and debrief, with the objective to improve the mission set.

Above: The USS *Carl Vinson* underway in the Philippine Sea with F-35C Lightning II aircraft assigned to Strike Fighter Squadron 147 on December 13, 2024. USN/ MC Seaman Apprentice Pablo Chavez

E-2D Hawkeye

CVW-8's forthcoming deployment will involve the debut of the E-2D Advanced Hawkeye aircraft. This is a significant system. According to Naval Air Systems Command, the E-2D Advanced Hawkeye features the state-of-the-art APY-9 active electronically scanned array radar to provide broad area coverage and command and control capability to co-ordinate concurrent missions that might arise during a single sortie to include airborne strike, land force support, rescue operations, managing a reliable communications network between widely dispersed nodes and support for drug interdiction operations. The use of the glass cockpit and tactical fourth operator display allows the five-person crew more flexibility in fulfilling these diverse missions. In addition to the probe, aerial refuelling-equipped aircraft feature new endurance seats, fuel system enhancements, and new exterior lighting.

The E-2D is at the centre of everything a CVW does based on the amount of information the aircraft is able to share. Its capability to exchange data is not limited to Link-16 and the CEC, but also radio systems, satellite communications, and computer network systems which can all exchange information with the carrier, the CAOC or any asset on the link.

In terms of aerial refuelling, E-2D pilots must plug 25 times to get their baseline currency, and then get qualified in aerial refuelling with various types of tanker.

COMPTUEX to Combat Operational Efficiency

Air Wing Fallon is followed by COMPTUEX in which aircrews use the skills learned at Fallon, integrate with all the ships in the CSG, and collectively fight from onboard the carrier.

COMPTUEX is tough training for all personnel. In the case of aircrew, they must carefully manage their aircraft's fuel state, get back to the carrier on time, recover on time while the deck remains open, so their aircraft can be quickly refuelled, rearmed, and re-launched to make the next tasking on time and the air boss must close the deck at a given time to enable the next cycle to launch. It's a complex process, with lots of moving parts, and requires a lot of planning and training. COMPTUEX is the essence of advanced integrated training with the ship and includes the dropping of ordnance.

According to the ship's assigned command, evaluators from either CSG-15 or CSG-4 check the air wing throughout COMPTUEX using many metrics.

Staff assigned to either CSG-15 or CSG-4 develop the scenarios and co-ordinate the assets that will challenge the CSG. The air wing fights collectively in a kill web comprising various elements from the CSG. It's not linear but dispersed and relies on the cruisers and destroyers assigned to the CSG which are intrinsic to success.

Upon successful completion of COMPTUEX, the CSG and the air wing will be certified with a combat operational efficiency (COE) score. This shows the air wing can efficiently launch off the flight deck and recover aircraft already airborne without the need for a divert airfield nearby. The air wing is required to meet established criteria of efficiency and safety during aircraft launch and recovery operations for nine consecutive days. Meteorological conditions for each flying day, classed as Case I, Case II, or Case III, are used to determine the air wing's COE score.

Case I occurs when flights are anticipated to not encounter instrument meteorological conditions (IMC) during daytime launches and recoveries, and the ceiling and visibility around the carrier are no lower than 3,000ft and 5nm, respectively. Maintaining radio silence during Case I launches and recoveries is normal, only breaking radio silence for safety-of-flight issues.

Case II occurs when flights may encounter IMC during daytime launches and recoveries, and the ceiling and visibility in the carrier control zone are no lower than 1,000ft and 5nm, respectively. It is used for an overcast condition.

Case III occurs when flights are expected to encounter IMC during launches and recoveries because the ceiling or visibility

Below: **An F-35C Lightning II, assigned to Strike Fighter Squadron 97, launches from the flight deck of the USS *Carl Vinson* in the US Central Command area of responsibility.** USN

around the carrier is lower than 1,000ft and 5nm, respectively, or for night-time launches and recoveries.

A calculation is made to generate a numbered COE score for the entire flight day, which determines whether the air wing has met the bar or not. COE certification is granted based on the air wing meeting the metric each day during the nine-day period.

Explaining the evaluation process to the editor, Captain Daryl Trent the former commander of CVW-8 said: "The challenges given to the CSG will not necessarily be an attack but something benign to see how we react. Remember the goal of an aircraft carrier is to deter, so the air wing is also evaluated on deterrence scenarios. In such events, evaluation considers if aircrew shot too quickly and demonstrated proficiency in understanding the rules of engagement? Each aircrew must pass that test, if they

don't, they don't fly. A pilot could shape the international stage based on a misunderstanding of what he or she was allowed to do.

"Some scenarios are benign on purpose to see if the aircrew react correctly. Do they go out and shoot? Are they too aggressive? That's debriefed ad nauseam, to make sure they fully understand that in such a situation they are authorised to employ weapons. In that event, they must explain to the air wing commander how they employed their weapon or more importantly why they did not employ their weapon? An air wing commander would much rather have aircrew leaning forward and reacting correctly as soon as the engagement threshold is met. That's what COMPTUEX trains you to do.

"As scenarios develop, if all unknown tracks are hostile, it's easy for the aircrew to engage, those are easy scenarios. A complicated scenario is one that involves

Below: Sailors signal to the pilot of an E-2D Hawkeye assigned to Airborne Command and Control Squadron 115 as ready to launch from the flight deck of USS *Theodore Roosevelt* underway in the 3rd Fleet area of operations on July 25, 2025. USN/MC 3C Aaron Haro Gonzalez

Above: **An F-35C Lightning II, from Strike Fighter Squadron 147 lands on the flight deck of the USS *George Washington* during carrier qualifications in December 2023.** USN/ MC3 August Clawson

what's referred to as white shipping or white air. They're neutral. A commercial aircraft or a third party that has nothing to do with the situation are in the wrong place at the wrong time. In such a scenario, do the aircrews understand how to effectively follow the rules of engagement? Employ the weapon appropriately? And at the right time? That is difficult."

Discussing the Houthi attacks on USN warships underway in the Red Sea at a Council on Foreign Relations panel discussion in Washington DC on May 19, 2025, Acting Chief of Naval Operations Admiral Jim Kilby said: "It's a fool's errand to think that the adversary is going to sit back and keep doing the same thing. They're going to change their tactics. So, we need to watch that and be very thoughtful about what is different, so we can prepare and be ready."

He continued: "The Truman strike group engaged 160 drones and missiles either heading to Israel or to them, or to defend commercial ships. The Truman strike group conducted 670 strikes and launched the largest air strike in the history, dropping 124,000lb of ordnance, from a single aircraft carrier into Somalia.

"Over a five-month period the Truman strike group worked for three different combatant commanders in the execution of its mission. That's flexibility. Following the big strike in Somalia, Operation Rough Rider involved an intensified campaign of strikes against Houthi targets in Yemen."

SERVING COD

The CMV-22B has served the US Navy for the best part of five years. Today it is deployed to the east and west coasts, and in Japan. Here is an overview of its service journey so far.

L OGISTICS SUPPORT TO US Navy (USN) carrier strike groups is currently fulfilled by the Grumman C-2A(R) Greyhound, a gutsy turboprop cargo aircraft introduced to fleet service in 1985.

For USN aircraft carriers and their assigned strike groups, the carrier onboard delivery (COD) role is critical. As the C-2A(R) retires, its place is being taken by a new type of aircraft – the tiltrotor CMV-22 Osprey – a machine that meets the official aerial resupply and logistics for sea basing requirements. It will provide the USN with operational capabilities and flexibilities not available from the Greyhound.

COD, the CMV-22B's primary mission, is officially defined as the use of aircraft to transport people and cargo from a forward logistics site (FLS) to a carrier strike group (CSG) at sea. Each FLS typically has two C-2 Greyhound aircraft assigned to conduct operations to and from the carrier.

Other missions tasked to the nascent CMV-22B are vertical on- board delivery (VOD), vertical replenishment (VERTREP, lifting supplies from one ship to another), medical evacuation (MEDEVAC), Naval special warfare, missions of state, humanitarian assistance/disaster relief, and search and rescue. Under the current plan, the Navy is due to receive 44 CMV- 22 aircraft.

A Navy Bird for a Navy mission

The CMV-22B is equipped with fuselage-sponsons housing more fuel cells (an MV-22's sponsons house a forward fuel cell on each side and one aft on the right hand side) which, combined with an additional fuel cell installed in each wing, increase the CMV-22B's total fuel load by an extra 815 gallons (5,540lb) to enable the CMV-22B to carry an additional 6,000lb of cargo over a range of 1,150nm out to or back from the ship. This is the only visual difference on the CMV-22B.

Certain component design changes had to be made to enable the large sponsons and the additional wing fuel tanks to be integrated in a CMV-22B. According to

Below: **A CMV-22B Osprey, assigned to Fleet Logistics Multi-Mission Squadron 40 lands on the flight deck of the USS *Gerald R Ford* during the first landing qualifications on a Ford-class aircraft carrier.** USN/MC2 Maxwell Orlosky

Bell-Boeing, the CMV- 22B configuration includes the addition of a left-hand and right-hand fuel cell in a previously dry bay in the mid-wing. The added fuel cell drove changes to the fuel management system. It also required new rollover valves and the re-qualification of breakaway valves.

The addition of the fuel cell into the previously empty wing bay required relocation of several existing systems, such as elements of the fire suppression system, hydraulic lines, and aircraft wiring.

Finally, there were changes to address structural reinforcement to support the new fuel cells as well as provisioning and penetrations to address system re-routing.

To meet the Navy's CMV-22 requirements, the V-22's baseline design required changes. Adjacent wing fuel cells were also redesigned to interface with the newly added fuel cell in the adjacent dry bay on the CMV-22B. The wing structure also received several sealant and corrosion preventative improvements to address water intrusion, such as a change from sealant to transfer tape which eliminated the need for a sealant cure time and allows for a cleaner removal.

Designing the CMV-22B offered additional opportunities for cost reduction and weight savings with the use of additive manufacturing, primarily in barrier clips, fuel cell cones, and spacers.

Other Navy-specific systems fitted are an HF radio for beyond line-of-sight

Above: **A sailor uses a forklift to load cargo onto a CMV-22B Osprey, assigned to Fleet Logistics Multi-Mission Squadron 30 on the flight deck of USS *Carl Vinson*.** USN/MC2 Jeff D Kempton

Right: **Sailors assigned to Fleet Logistics Multi-Mission Squadron 40 and air department aboard the USS *Gerald R Ford*, chock and chain a CMV-22B Osprey to the flight deck during aircraft carrier qualifications.** USN/MC Seaman Tajh Payne

communications, a passenger public address system and a revised cabin lighting configuration for safe loading and unloading of cargo during nighttime operations.

CMV-22B also has a baseline receiver-only aerial refuelling capability installed, to further extend range when required.

Aircraft survivability equipment includes the ubiquitous AAR-47 missile warning set, the ALE-47 countermeasure dispensing system, and the APR-39A radar signals detection set.

The CMV-22B's FLIR imaging is generated by a mid-wavelength infrared AAQ-27 sensor.

Production

Boeing builds the new sponsons in its state-of-the-art composite facility at Philadelphia where the larger tanks, internal fuel cells and the additional aft sponson tank are installed on the line. The wing fuel cells require new computer numerical control machine programming to trim new access holes and penetrations into the existing V-22 spar design, all of which is undertaken at Bell's Fort Worth composite centre. Installation is undertaken on the assembly line at Bell's Amarillo facility. According to Bell, V-22

subassembly and structure build are both impacted by the changes which increase the build time of the CMV-22B's wing. Human factors, pre-fitting components, drilling of 90-plus holes, shimming with epoxy, and faying surface sealing all contribute to the new build time. From an overall final assembly timeline perspective, there are no major changes in aircraft sequencing on the Amarillo line because all the CMV-22B's major dynamic and structural components are identical to the other V-22 variants.

However, minor new and modified tooling changes had to be made at two positions to accommodate the larger sponsons. Holding fixtures, a layup tool, numerical control, and ply cutting programs are some examples. Neither does installation of the additional wing fuel cell require a sequencing change, though some minor changes also had to be made to the assembly functional test plan, and the equivalent used for flight test.

Range Perfect

Longer range strike missiles continue to proliferate around the world, none more so than those in the arsenals of China and Russia. China fields the Dong Feng 21D (DF-21D) ballistic missile with a range that exceeds 800nm (1,500km), while Russia's

Kh-47M2 Kinzhal (Dagger) air-launched ballistic missile has a reported range of 1,100nm launched from a MiG-31K and a whopping 1,600nm when punched off a Tu-22M3 *Blinder*.

What do facts about ballistic missiles have to do with the CMV- 22B Osprey? The answer is range. USN carrier strike groups no longer operate with the level of impunity once enjoyed in past decades and would have to remain further away from a hostile coastline to stay outside of an adversary's missile engagement zone. The distance depends on the type of missile faced, but in some scenarios over 1,000 miles.

Consequently, the CMV-22B has a payload-range mix far more than the current C-2A(R). In tropical conditions, at a 1,150nm (2,000km) range the CMV-22B can haul 6,000lb compared to the C-2's 5,600lb. That's a key operational requirement to ensure a carrier can remain outside of threat missile engagement zones and within range of the shore base when operating from an FLS. Given the CMV-22B has an aerial refuelling capability, the tiltrotor's range can be further extended when tanker support is available. With just one aerial refuelling, a CMV-22B can fly for another 500-700nm depending on payload.

Above: **Sailors assigned to Fleet Logistics Multi-Mission Squadron 40 and air department chock and chain a CMV-22B Osprey during the type's first carrier qualifications in September 2024.** USN/MC Seaman Tajh Payne

While it has the capability to land and take-off with sidestep procedures, this increases risk of downwash and limits the aircraft gross weight capabilities within its operating envelope. Consequently, the CMV-22B will operate as a fixed-wing aircraft for recoveries, entering the standard pattern and fly normal fixed wing VFR/IFR recovery procedures at the carrier. This will culminate in an approach and no-hover landing up the stern of the ship, lined up with the landing area centreline. This procedure has already been exercised during multiple at-sea CVN periods, and has proven to be the most efficient, safe, and expeditious recovery of the

V-22 with the other types of aircraft in the carrier air wing. In fact, the Osprey's pattern airspeed (170 KCAS – knots calibrated airspeed – in airplane mode) is compatible with fixed wing jet and turboprop aircraft within the air wing.

"The ability of the tiltrotor aircraft to integrate with fixed-wing operations, and also operate at night, will give the CVN a new level of flexibility to adjust operations however required to accomplish the mission," Chaney explained.

"For short turnarounds, the aircraft will use the normal tie down chains and chocks required for all ship-board aircraft. The CMV-22B has several hard-points located on the underside and side of the fuselage which are the attachment points for the hooks of the tie-down chains. Once the aircraft lands, the taxi director will pass directional control of the aircraft to the deck crew to chock and chain the aircraft. Once that is complete, the pilot will be

Below: **Sailors load cargo into a CMV-22B Osprey, attached to Fleet Logistics Multi-Mission Squadron 30 on the flight deck of the USS *Carl Vinson* in the US Central Command area of responsibility.** USN

cleared to reduce engine rpm to place the aircraft in an idle configuration.

"Another option for longer on-deck periods will be to shut down the main engines leaving only the APU running. After loading is complete and the aircraft is ready to depart, flight deck control will clear the deck crew to remove the chocks and chains. At that point, the pilot will receive clearance to increase engine rpm to bring all systems up for flight."

Fleet Activity

Fleet Logistics Multi-Mission Wing (VRMWING) is established at Naval Air Station North Island, California, as the type wing responsible for manning, training, and equipment for all the eventual CMV-22B operational and training squadrons.

Fleet Logistics Multi-Mission Squadron 30 (VRM-30) 'Titans' is also established at North

Island, as is VRM-50 the Fleet Replacement Squadron established in October 2020, a forward deployed detachment overseas, VRM-30 FDNF is based at MCAS Iwakuni Japan, and the second operational squadron VRM-40 is based at Naval Station Norfolk, Virginia.

USN training is focused on carrier strike group logistics, and long–range missions in support of aircraft carriers and follows a specific fleet training model.

Because the V-22 was already proven as a viable platform aboard ship, Air Test and Evaluation Squadron 1, NAVAIR's operational test squadron, supported by VRM-30, tested the differences between the CMV-22B and the data already held about the MV-22.

For its first deployment, VRM-30 was only required to deploy one detachment in support of theatre security operations, a requirement that could for the most part be filled by the existing MV-22 capability. Full operational capability required the CMV-22B to demonstrate its unique range and force integration capabilities, and the ability to support combat operations.

Initial Operational Capability

The CMV-22B's initial operational capability (IOC) declaration was made on December 14, 2021, two months before the type's maiden deployment ended in mid-February 2022.

During the summer of 2021 three CMV-22Bs assigned to a detachment from VRM-30 embarked on the USS *Carl Vinson* as part of CVW-2 for a six-month deployment.

Above: **A CVM-22B Osprey assigned to Fleet Logistics Multi-Mission Squadron 40 prepares to land on the flight deck of the USS *George H W Bush*.** USN/MC2 Nicholas Avis

GREYHOUND AND OSPREY CHARACTERISTICS

	C-2A(R) Greyhound	CMV-22B Osprey
Crew	Two pilots, two aircrew	Two pilots, two aircrew
Max pax	26	24
Max payload	10,000lb (4,535kg)	20,000lb (9,070kg)
Cargo space	872ft³ (24.7m³)	739ft³ (20.9m³)
Max speed	343kts	280kts
Cruise speed	251kts	241kts
Range	1,000nm	1,150nm
Service ceiling	30,000ft	25,000ft

Above: **A CVM-22B Osprey prepares to land on the flight deck of the USS *George HW Bush* underway in the Atlantic Ocean.** USN/MC2 Nicholas Avis

needed for carrier delivery operations," Williamson said.

"There are very few flight hours on the initial CMV-22 aircraft we'll be receiving, so they're essentially in new condition. We presume the work scope will build in the future, based on the harsh shipborne operating environment, and a high utilisation rate.

"Guidance will give the [production] team the opportunity to look at the aircraft and its needs with fresh eyes, rather than with pre-existing expectations… With the first aircraft, we're emphasising to the team that they should take their time and really explore whether there are any additional differences in the aircraft itself, of the way we work it versus how we would work an MV. The biggest difference in CMV-22B depot-level maintenance appears be the aircraft's paint job."

Commenting on the paint scheme, FRCE's Paint and Clean branch head Matt Sinsel said: "The aircraft uses a high-gloss paint, so the prep and the application are going to be a little bit different than what we're used to with the standard MV-22B. There will be some differences in the masking process because the paint scheme is a little higher-profile than the standard grey Ospreys.

"The CMV-22B's unique paint scheme also gives the team another opportunity to use the laser projection system the depot began using in January to streamline the final finish process, during which an aircraft's insignia and other markings are applied to the finished base paint. The system acts as a guide for the precise placement of the markings without having to use paper stencils."

Discussing the FRCE's track record of working on V-22 aircraft, Williamson said: "We're known for what we do, and not just within the brick-and-mortar site at Cherry Point. We have our detachment at New River, which is revered in its own light for the way they conduct a PMI. We have the in-service repair team at New River that is making depot-level repairs while embedded with the marine VMM squadrons, and we have a detachment Hurlburt Field in Florida, where we support Air Force Special Operations Command."

V-22 Prop-Rotor Gear Box and a Grounding

On November 29, 2023, Air Force Special Operations Command CV-22B Osprey, serial number 10-0054, assigned to the 21st Special Operations Squadron based at Yokota Air Base, Japan, impacted the water half a mile off the coast of Yakushima Island, while on approach to Yakushima Airport.

The US Air Force Accident Investigation Board identified a catastrophic failure of the left-hand proprotor gearbox (PRGB) which caused instant asymmetric lift, which made the aircraft roll twice before impacting the water.

The CV-22B aircraft was destroyed, and all eight crewmembers were killed. Consequently, the V-22 fleet was grounded until the entire US fleet was cleared to fly again with new restrictions issued in an interim flight clearance (IFC)

on March 8, 2024, The US Air Force Accident Investigation Board issued its report on the accident, on August 1, 2024.

Flight safety concerns re-emerged after an Air Force Special Operations Command CV-22B made a performed precautionary landing on November 20, 2024, during a local training mission from Cannon Air Force Base, New Mexico which led to an operational pause for all V-22 variants.

One month later, NAVAIR issued a fleet bulletin directing an inspection of V-22 Osprey aircraft to verify the flight hours on each PRGB prior to an aircraft's next flight.

V-22 aircraft with PRGBs that currently met or exceeded a pre-determined flight-hour threshold would resume flights in accordance with controls instituted in the March 2024 IFC.

A new IFC, containing additional risk mitigation controls, was issued to address aircraft with PRGBs below the flight-hour threshold. These controls remain in place until the aircraft's PRGBs are upgraded, or the predetermined threshold is exceeded.

First Time on Deck

VRM-40 made history on March 18, 2025, when one of its assigned CMV-22Bs landed aboard USS *George HW Bush* (CVN 77) for the first time.

Describing the event in a press release, Lieutenant David Turner, a CMV-22B pilot with VRM-40 said: "Being the first [CMV-22B squadron assigned to the Atlantic fleet] and starting from scratch

is definitely a challenge. When you are the first to ever do something, you get to find all the problems, and it's your responsibility to fix and learn from them for the benefit of those who follow you."

VRM-40 was established at Naval Air Station North Island, California, but relocated to Naval Station Norfolk on February 1, 2024.

Discussing the move from California to Virginia, Turner said: "It was a long road to transfer from West coast to East coast operations. We had to completely transfer our whole squadron and faced numerous logistic and platform-specific challenges."

To prepare for the first deck landing on the *Bush*, VRM-40 worked on its operations with the ship and its carrier strike group. Commenting on the preparations, Adam Nagi, a naval aircrewman with VRM-40, said: "Collaboration is important because the better the communication is between the squadron and the strike group, the more smoothly we can get logistics and high priority personnel on and off the ship. Teamwork is integral to how our squadron operates alongside our surface ship counterparts to make sure all our joint operations go to plan."

CMV-22B Virtues, C-2A Retirement

Discussing the CMV-22B's first deployment embarked on the USS *Carl Vinson* at an event on maritime security hosted by the Center for Strategic and International Studies and the US Naval Institute in July

2022, Vice Admiral Kenneth Whitesell, then Commander of Naval Air Forces and Naval Air Force, US Pacific Fleet, said: "With distributed maritime ops, longer ranges, distances between multi-carrier operations, distances from land-based areas, and the ability for the CMV-22B to land on unimproved spaces, it proved to be a game-changer for us on deployment."

When the V-22 fleet was grounded on December 6, 2023, Carrier Air Wing 2 was embarked on the USS *Carl Vinson* with three CMV-22Bs assigned to North Island-based VRM-30 Det 1, the second deployment involving the type. The need for carrier onboard delivery necessitated the embarkation of two C-2A(R) Greyhounds assigned to VRC-40 Det 5 which joined the ship from Iwakuni, Japan.

Subsequent carriers that departed US waters were the USS *Theodore Roosevelt* (CVN 71) in January 2024 with CVW-11 embarked including C-2A(R) Greyhounds assigned to VRC-40 Det 3, followed in July by the USS *Abraham Lincoln* (CVN 72) with CVW-9 embarked including C-2(AR) Greyhounds assigned to VRC-40 Det 2.

Approximately 12 C-2A(R) Greyhound aircraft are assigned to VRC-40 based at Naval Air Station Norfolk, which were supporting carriers assigned to both the Atlantic and Pacific fleets while the V-22 grounding remained in effect. The last of C-2A(R) aircraft is currently scheduled to retire in August 2026. The USN plans to acquire 48 aircraft across all VRM squadrons.

Below: **A CMV-22B Osprey, assigned to VRM-30 takes off from the flight deck of the USS *Carl Vinson* during routine operations in the 7th Fleet area of operations.** USN/MC2 Isaiah B Goessl

PATROL SQUADRON X

An insight into the operations of a P-8A Poseidon-equipped patrol squadron.

LIKE MOST US Navy (USN) aircraft squadrons, a patrol squadron comprises departments including admin, command services, tactics, safety and ETOPS (extended operations performance standards), training, operations, and maintenance, all manned by support personnel, aircrew, and maintainers.

A patrol squadron's lifecycle between deployment follows a 12-month Fleet Response Training Plan (FRTP) between deployment cycles. The FRTP is designed to enhance readiness and streamline deployment cycles. It involves a structured approach to maintenance, training, and deployment and has four phases: maintenance, basic, advanced, and integrated. When the squadron returns from deployment it enters the basic phase for six months of the FRTP, then enters the advanced phase, when it garners the last qualifications required for deployment certification.

A squadron undergoes several inspections as part of its certification process, for example a maintenance programme assessment conducted by staff from the squadron's parent wing followed by an aviation maintenance inspection conducted by a team from Commander, Naval Air Forces which awards the final certification to the maintenance department.

Another is focused on weapons and known as the Conventional Weapons Technical Proficiency Inspection (CWTPI) which assesses the squadron's ability to handle and maintain conventional weapons systems. CWTPI is conducted by a team from the maritime patrol weapons school based at Naval Air Station Jacksonville, Florida. The team ensures that the squadron's aviation ordnance men follow all procedures properly, when assembling, handling, loading, arming, disarming sonar buoys and weapons on the aircraft. As part of the inspection the team flies onboard an aircraft to ensure the crew follows the release procedures correctly when employing the weapon.

Live fire events involving AGM-84 Harpoon missiles and Mk54 torpedoes occur at different points in time during the squadron's home cycle. Firing live Harpoon missiles can occur during deployment, during a stint at Keflavik Air Base, Iceland, the crew of a P-8 aircraft fired a Harpoon missile on a weapons range in the Hebrides.

Above: **A P-8A Poseidon assigned to Patrol Squadron 46 (VP-46) at Keflavik Air Base, on July 24, 2025.** USN/Lt Sara Wedemeyer

Below: **A P-8A Poseidon assigned to Patrol Squadron 46 (VP-46) takes off from runway 32 at Naval Air Station Whidbey Island, Washington during work-up to deployment to the US 6th Fleet areas of operation.** USN/Lt Sara Wedemeyer

A programme called Naval Air Training and Operating Procedures Standardization or NATOPS establishes standardised flight and operating procedures for all naval aircraft. The programme aims to improve combat readiness and reduce aircraft mishaps. A squadron's compliance with NATOPS is evaluated by a team from Patrol Squadron 30 (VP-30) based at Naval Air Station Jacksonville, Florida. A team from VP-30 visits the squadron to administer an annual exam taken by each aircrewman and fly a check ride for each of the squadron's NATOPS instructors. A squadron NATOPS Instructor is a highly qualified aircrew member assigned to the squadron whose primary or secondary duty is administering the NATOPS programme. They are responsible for conducting positional upgrade and/or annual periodic check rides for flight crew, ensuring adherence to NATOPS procedures and maintaining standardisation within the squadron.

The capstone event in a squadron's certification process is an operational readiness evaluation, which is a comprehensive assessment to ensure the squadron is prepared for deployment and capable of performing its mission in various operational environments. An ORE is a full-scale demonstration of the squadron's ability to deliver critical capabilities, such as combat readiness, under challenging conditions.

An ORE Involves a simulator phase, conducted by an inspector from a board of inspection and survey from the squadron's parent wing, who evaluates aircrew during different scenarios matched to deployment locations to ensure their ability to accomplish a mission. The ORE also involves a flight phase, in which every aircrew conducts a flight event with an inspector onboard to ensure the mission can be executed, it represents the pinnacle of operational valuation for aircrew. The squadron's maintenance department plays a big role in the ORE flight phase by ensuring each aircraft is ready for scheduled flight events.

Once the ORE is signed off, additional readiness qualifications must be met, each based on the squadron's remaining currency to support each mission set: anti-submarine warfare, anti-surface warfare and intelligence, surveillance, and reconnaissance. Once all readiness qualifications are successfully completed, the wing's Commodore can request a formal deployment certification from the Admiral at Commander, Naval Air Force, which allows the squadron to deploy.

Once the formal deployment certification is issued, the squadron is briefed on its expected deployment location in Europe, Southwest Asia, Japan, or elsewhere. No matter what destination, the squadron's qualifications are standard and suitable for all deployment locations and potential adversaries.

Visitors on the Wing

There have been many occasions recently when USN P-8 Poseidon aircraft have had unannounced company on the wing during a patrol flight in international airspace. Generally, the unannounced company is Chinese or Russian fighter aircraft, some of which have flown dangerously close to the P-8 aircraft. In preparation for such scenarios, P-8 aircrews use intercept training opportunities with USN fighters and those from the other services to experience what an aircraft looks like when 100 or 50ft away. The actions conducted by Chinese and Russian fighters place a lot

of emphasis on interception training and generates lots of discussion. In the event of a non-standard interaction, P-8 aircrews must know what normal looks like and be prepared for an abnormal interaction.

Anti-Submarine Warfare

A P-8 aircraft can operate anywhere and in an expeditionary nature. Anti-submarine warfare (ASW) is its primary mission one that is conducted operating from numerous bases located around the world, including some allied bases such as RAF Lossiemouth in Scotland.

ASW missions last for several hours, submarines tend to operate in remote areas of the world's oceans, so P-8 aircrews are faced with long transits to and from the area of interest. Aerial refuelling capability increases the aircraft's endurance and stay airborne longer in support of the mission.

The mission crew uses different resources to find a submarine.

Passive buoys detect acoustic signals without emitting any sound itself. Directional Command Active Sonobuoy Systems (DICASS) active buoys detect and localise submarines using active sonar, providing range, and bearing information for attack planning. Multi-static coherent active buoys are part of a system that uses multiple sonobuoys, some acting as sound sources and others as receivers, to detect and locate submarines.

The mix of buoys used is based on the water environment, the intelligence briefed to the crew ahead of the mission, and the intended target, which combined, allow the crew to define the

Above: **Sailors assigned to Patrol Squadron 5 (VP-5) conduct routine maintenance on a wing of a P-8A Poseidon aircraft in the hangar at Naval Air Station Sigonella, Sicily.** USN/MC2 Sang Kim

target. Acoustic operators are trained to recognise the acoustic signatures of different types of submarines.

As the information comes to the aircraft from the acoustic system, the acoustic operators can quickly call out a classifying frequency or characteristic that is only associated with the specific submarine under search, which is a unique skill set.

The way that the target operates, the tactics it employs, and the different techniques it uses to evade and beat the crew's search efforts, drives how the crew specifically employs the aircraft to successfully maintain tracking of the submarine.

What happens next depends on the commander's intent and specifics of the mission. If the mission objective has been met, the crew breaks contact and returns to base. If the mission objective is not complete, the crew will hand over the tasking to another aircraft to maintain a continuous track.

The aircraft's operating environment, in terms of ocean temperature, water depth, and the weather, all impact on the effectiveness or not of the aircraft and the mission crew. Shipping traffic and sea life, for example, can increase the ambient noise level in the water which makes it more

Right: **An aviation structural mechanic airman assigned to Patrol Squadron 5 (VP-5) conducts routine maintenance on a rear horizontal stabiliser of a P-8A Poseidon aircraft in the hangar at Naval Air Station Sigonella, Sicily.** USN/MC2 Sang Kim

challenging for the mission crew to detect a specific acoustic signature of a submarine.

Some water columns favour certain sensors over others. Aircrew are trained to ensure the mission crew can use the best tactics and the best sensors to take advantage of the water column. Seasonal changes affect the water column but day-to-day, an operator familiar with the water column will notice minor adjustments.

Anti-Surface Warfare

Anti-surface warfare (ASuW) focusses on attacking and neutralising adversary surface ships with a range of weapons, sensors, and tactics, including the P-8 aircraft.

The mission crew uses the APY-10 radar, the aircraft's primary sensor, to detect surface traffic using its search mode, or the inverse synthetic aperture radar mode for ships at long range. The passive ESM (electronic support measures) system can also be used to detect emissions coming from a target ship the mission crew wants to detect and identify.

The aircrew can employ the aircraft to minimise its detection, some of the

Above: A P-8A Poseidon on a routine mission over the US Central Command area of responsibility, May 31, 2025.
USAF/SrA Keegan Putman

sensors enable target detection at greater standoff ranges. The environment also plays a factor. Different types of refractive ducts present themselves based on the environmental conditions that allow for a detection at much farther than a normal range.

Refractive ducts, also known as atmospheric ducts, is a phenomenon

Right: A P-8A assigned to Patrol Squadron 46 (VP-46) at Naval Air Station Whidbey Island, Washington, on April 1, 2025.
USN/Lt Sara Wedemeyer

in the Earth's atmosphere where radio waves or light signals are trapped due to specific atmospheric conditions in which the refractive index decreases rapidly with height, causing radio waves to bend downwards and become confined within a layer. These ducts can significantly impact long-distance communication and radar systems by either enhancing or interfering with signal propagation.

For instance, the typical range on a day might be 50 miles, but if a duct is involved, range could double or triple because the radar returns travel longer distances because it is trapped in a duct above sea level. Ducts can be used to the mission crew's advantage to detect something from further away, but also can result in greater detection by the target.

The ISR role (intelligence, surveillance, and reconnaissance) is conducted over water and overland using the EO/IR camera and or the APY-10 radar. The radar's synthetic aperture mode is specifically aimed at mapping out targets and can be used overland.

Training

Because anti-sub warfare is the primary mission for a patrol squadron it occupies the propensity of a squadron's training, with ASuW and ISR occupying the rest.

Opportunities to conduct pilot training, with dedicated time to focus on pilot upgrades that must be completed, which are harder to come by on deployment due to operational requirements. Several pilot training events are accomplished in a simulator.

Different ratings' qualifications must also be completed to deploy and are generally

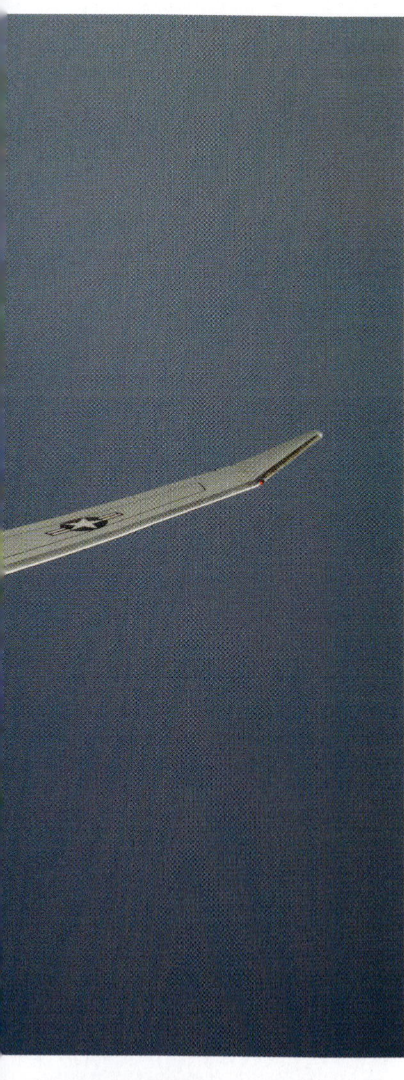

completed on training events with other US forces.

During each squadron upcycle, each crew must complete a torpedo exercise, which involves employing an inert torpedo on a weapons sea range, typically near San Diego or Hawaii.

A patrol squadron must also stage coordinated ASW operations, and coordinated ASuW operations for a range of qualifications that must be achieved. These events require involvement of other assets.

A carrier strike group does not have readiness requirements that involve P-8, but the aircraft remains a key player in the carrier's training events with its long-range ASW capability.

Additional training opportunities for working with a carrier strike group manifest throughout a patrol squadron's home cycle in a variety of regular training exercises, some of which require the capabilities only available from a P-8.

However, participation in the submarine commander's course is probably the most enjoyable exercise for a P-8 squadron to be involved with. Prospective submarine commanders undertake the rigorous courses, during which they fight P-8s and do everything possible to evade detection. A liaison officer from the submarine force tells the P-8 crew the

Below: **An aircrewman operator assigned to Patrol Squadron 46 (VP-46) handles a sonobuoy inside a P-8A Poseidon flying over the Norwegian Sea, May 8, 2025, during Dynamic Mongoose 2025, a NATO-led advanced anti-submarine warfare exercise.** USN/MC2 Jacquelin Frost

objectives for each specific vignette, because they change as the course evolves. Typically, the mission crew tries to challenge the submarine commander by doing things to make life as difficult as possible for him. The P-8 employs the aircraft in any way possible to maintain track and force the submarine commander to use everything they have at their disposal to evade the aircraft. Post-mission, the liaison officer feeds the lessons learned back to the aircraft crew.

Aircraft Improvements

The P-8 Poseidon follows an incremental upgrade process designed to field upgrades to the fleet as quickly as possible. The aircraft in fleet service today have improved significantly compared to the first P-8 aircraft delivered to Patrol Squadron 30 (VP-30), the training squadron, in 2012.

Steady progress in fixing issues and making small incremental improvements to the capabilities in each software release are significant to the mission crew. Software improvements, for example, provide more capability and give operators more options to choose from, more integration between systems and more flexibility with them.

The way the aircraft is operated on station, being GPS-enabled, the aircraft's ability to maintain good plots, and for the crew to know the aircraft's position accurately especially at mid-ocean locations, and the ability to maintain position, which enables the aircraft to operate at higher altitudes and the mission crew to where a given submarine is during its prosecution are examples of beneficial capabilities.

Right: **A P-8A Poseidon approaches a US Air Force KC-135R Stratotanker for aerial refueling over the US Central Command area of responsibility, May 31, 2025.** USAF/SrA Keegan Putman

Right: **An aircrewman assigned to Patrol Squadron 45 (VP-45) works at the console aboard a P-8A Poseidon on a mission in support of Breeze 2024, an anti-submarine warfare and maritime interdiction exercise led by the Bulgarian navy.** USN/ MC2 Jonathan Berlier

Below: **A P-8A Poseidon assigned to Patrol Squadron 46 (VP-46) takes off from Naval Air Station Whidbey Island, Washington.** USN/Lt Sara Wedemeyer

Deployments

As mentioned earlier, patrol squadrons undertake regular six-month deployments to Europe, Southwest Asia, and Japan. During such a deployment the squadron conducts operational missions, as directed by the commander of a Combined Task Force, and participates in exercises. Some exercises are focused on training with allies, others are focused on partnerships to demonstrate the ability to work with nations that may not be in NATO but benefit from the training and learn from each other.

When deployed to the European 6th Fleet area, the squadron operates from different locations, with its aircraft moving around those locations as driven by operational requirements.